SITUATION SKIING

SITUATION SKIING

JEAN-CLAUDE KILLY
with Mike Halstead

Photographs by John C. Russell

1978

DOUBLEDAY & COMPANY, INC./GARDEN CITY, NEW YORK

Library of Congress Cataloging in Publication Data

Killy, Jean Claude.
Situation skiing.

1. Skis and skiing. I. Halstead, Mike, joint author.
II. Title.
GV854.K495   796.9'3
ISBN: 0-385-12189-x
Library of Congress Catalog Card Number 77–16927

Designed by Joseph P. Ascherl

Portions of this book appeared in the
magazine *Ski* as SKI MY WAY . . . . . AND NEVER
GET TIRED and SKIING IS ALL IN YOUR HEAD!,
Copyright Jean-Claude Killy and Mike Halstead, 1977, and
SITUATION SKIING, Copyright © International Literary Management, 1976.

PREFACE

I have known Jean-Claude Killy for over ten years: five as a fan, one as a fellow competitor on the pro tour (he won that year and still refers to me as "the only amateur on that year's tour"), and five as the person who looks after his North American business interests, and increasingly, a pretty good friend.

The development of *Situation Skiing* makes quite a story in itself. It all started when our literary agent approached several publishers with the concept of a safe-driving book by Jackie Stewart. This idea appealed to Doubleday's Sandy Richardson, but not nearly as much as a book on safe skiing by Jean-Claude Killy.

When it looked as though the project would be approved, I approached Jean-Claude, only to discover that he had "had it" with ghost-written literary projects. In short, he was fed up with spending one or two weeks confined with someone he did not know, and have the end product bear little or no resemblance to the input. "I'll tell you what," he said. "You are a good writer" (I guess he liked the way I had been preparing the itineraries for his trips to the States) "and you are certainly familiar with the way I think; I'll do it if you write it. Besides, it will give you an excuse to come to Val d'Isere this summer for some cycling and some glacier skiing!"

Little did I know that more than once before the conclusion of this project, I would look at Jean-Claude with some exasperation and utter the following Laurel and Hardyism: "Well, here's another fine mess you've gotten me into!"

Cut to Geneva: Following a little glacier skiing, a great deal of cycling around the French countryside with Jean-Claude and some fellow fanatics, and several afternoon skull sessions on the sundeck of Jean-Claude's home, we produced what our publisher feared would be little more than a glamorous version of a National Ski Patrol manual on safe skiing. It was at this point that we sat down, took a hard look at the existing mass of skiing literature, and determined that what was really needed was a book for the thinking skier—a book that would provide everything one has to know to get the most out of his or her skiing experience, regardless of level of proficiency. Perhaps more importantly, the skiing world needs a book of this type written in language everyone can understand and presented in a format that will take the philosophies and wealth of knowledge of the world's greatest skier and drive them home to the layman in a way in which they will be easily incorporated into his skiing repertoire.

Add to this a memorable and enjoyable week-long photo session with one of the world's great ski photographers, John C. Russell, and a year and a half of part-time but nevertheless exhaustive collaborative effort on the part of author and writer, and *voilà:* Another fine mess? We hope not!

MICHAEL W. HALSTEAD, *New York City, Winter 1978*

CONTENTS

Introduction

THE JOY OF SKIING

I am often asked whether, as the result of my many years as a competitor, or my many commercial involvements in skiing, I ever get tired of the sport. My answer: an unequivocal NO! Why? Because I enjoy it; it's as simple as that. Actually, my reasons are a bit more complex, and if you have a few minutes and are interested, I will outline a few of the reasons why skiing is an activity that transcends sport or hobby and in many cases becomes a way of life unto itself.

To begin with, skiing is a sport with a lifetime application, an activity that, if properly approached, can be enjoyed at different paces and in varying degrees by persons from 3 to 103 (these are arbitrary numbers, although I have known skiers of both ages). Second, skiing has tremendous value as a social activity. It allows for independent activity on the part of the individual during the day and shared group activity during breaks as well as the multiplicity of *après*-ski activities that await the energetic at day's end.

Skiing provides an unparalleled feeling of independence. It is a sport in which one can go at his or her own pace, independent of machinery or, for that matter, other people, since you do not need a partner to go skiing. Even on the most crowded of mountains, you can find a place for solitude. Granted, you must sometimes be prepared to sacrifice for this luxury—for example, by skiing in the shade when the crowds are in the sun.

Skiing provides an element of freedom—of exhilarating liberation—not present in most other athletic endeavors. In skiing, you cut your own swath, unconfined by track or court. With this freedom comes mobility, the power to cover amazing distances in a short amount of time without the aid of machinery. In my hometown of Val d'Isere, for example, I can, depending, of course, on the time I spend in lift lines, travel in a matter of just a few minutes, from one point to another several miles and three mountains away.

For me, one of the most enjoyable aspects of skiing is derived through the rather unique communication between the skier and his equipment. You may dismiss this as an idiosyncrasy of a purist. Perhaps you are right; in my second love, cycling, I would estimate that 30 per cent of my pleasure is received from the bike itself. Similarly, in skiing, I derive a great amount of satisfaction from having smooth bottoms and finely tuned edges on my skis, the right pair of skis for what I want to do, and so on.

For many, myself included, skiing can provide a powerful pathway to personal development. I have found that by challenging myself on the slopes and winning, I have been able to overcome hangups that were retarding my development in other areas of my life. Skiing, I have found, has physical and emotional cleansing properties. By forcing one to focus one's attention on a limited number of things—with pause for reflection between runs—this sport seems to produce a mind-clearing, almost meditative, effect. I have also learned that due to the variety of circumstances that I encounter and to which I must react while skiing, the sport has contributed greatly to the development of my decision-making abilities. Temperature, I have found, plays an important role as well. It has been my observation that the "Big Cold," as I call it, also helps clear the mind. When I was racing, I noticed that the colder the temperature, the faster and more precise were my reactions, perhaps as a by-product of my subconscious psychological and physiological preparation for this adverse environmental situation. I know doctors, lawyers, and businesspeople who, although they arrive at the ski area after an epic journey and totally exhausted from their grind at the office, amazingly muster the necessary energy to ski hard from nine o'clock in the morning to four o'clock in the afternoon, claiming that this is made possible largely by the refreshing properties of skiing fast in the cold air—both of which should exhaust rather than refresh. Although I am sure that there are other factors involved, the clear, crisp environment and the brisk temperatures must provide at least a psychological motivation for these weekend warriors.

Although there are varying theories on the role of our sport vis-à-vis mental health, there can be no doubt that, apart from the odd broken bone or stretched ligament, skiing provides a healthy cardiovascular workout in the fresh air and sunshine—something hard to find during those dreary winter months and something that cannot help but have a positive effect on your general well-being. Skiing seems to benefit the entire body. In skiing, you do many things that require and develop strength (not muscle size), balance, endurance, and agility.

I have found that skiing, unlike practically any other sport, is an activity in which, without thinking about it, you can push yourself to extraordinary levels of physical activity—and enjoy it. Skiing, unlike most sports, is practiced on an incline, and by its very nature, forces you to keep making rather physically demanding moves—or else! If you are running around the park, you can always find an excuse to slow down; but not so when you are traveling down a slippery piste at a high rate of speed. I am sure that this "danger" element in skiing generates an extraordinary flow of adrenaline, which makes possible moves that expand your physical and mental abilities with considerably more ease than would be the case in other forms of physical activity. Funny as it may sound, skiing is a sport in which even though you feel like you have been beaten to death after the first day, you still feel good. This applies to skiers of all levels, including yours truly.

Skiing is replete with cultural benefits as well. When you start skiing, you not only take up a sport; you adopt a new and distinct lifestyle. Over the years, I have observed that people have a tendency to become liberated at the ski resort—to act and dress differently than they do in their everyday lives. A couple of observations on dress: nine out of ten women look good in stretch pants—that is certainly more than you can say with regard to bikinis at the beach! And if you are wearing tight pants, a racing jacket, and heavy boots, you know that you are doing something special. In a way, these unique cosmetics of skiing in themselves provide a refreshing escape from one's day-to-day routine.

As I said, skiing is more than a sport; it is rather a distinct subculture. The warmth and ambience of the ski resort inspire a camaraderie that does not ordinarily exist among people. Skiing is a great equalizer. It does not matter who you are—the mailboy or the chairman of the board—you are all the same at the ski resort: You are skiers—people up there to have fun skiing and enjoying the nightlife with no ulterior motives. In short, a poor man can get tan just as fast and turn just as well as a rich one. Throughout the course of my professional career, I have seen even the most hardened cynics fall in love with the aspects of skiing of which I now speak. I have seen experienced business people become involved in skiing (as part of their jobs through what to them started out as a routine promotional program) and suddenly become zealous, almost dogmatic devotees of highly specialized forms of skiing such as ski racing or freestyle skiing. It was not racing or freestyle that they fell in love with, but the charm and exhilaration of the sport as a whole. In writing this, it occurred to me that the national slogan of France pretty well describes the essence of life in a ski resort: "Liberty, Equality, Fraternity."

Apart from physical and emotional dividends one derives from the activity itself, and the pleasurable ambience of the ski resort and subculture, one of skiing's greatest benefits lies in the fact that it takes you to many beautiful places to which you would not normally go. From the wooded ski trails of New England to the awe-inspiring alpine peaks of the Rockies, skiing unfolds a panoply of exotic, stimulating, and ever-changing environments. Skiing not only takes you to places you would not normally go (the most obvious being the tops of mountains), but also has a great international following, which enables you to meet people from many nations and interact with them on a common basis, relating to them first as skiers and second as Americans, Austrians, French, etc. How many people you know would go to Europe just to play tennis? With skiing it is different. With each new mountain comes a totally new adventure. Tennis courts are the same the world over, but with skiing a good part of the fun comes from experiencing and conquering new terrain.

Skiing not only provides diversity from nation to nation, and mountain to mountain, but also an environment so dynamic that great differences in temperature, topography, and snow conditions can exist on a single mountain on a single day. It is this ever-present challenge from changing conditions that provides for me the greatest thrills of the sport, and even I can find challenge on any hill or mountain in the world.

People often tell me that they would never take up skiing because they are too old, or they do not want to look stupid, or that skiing is too dangerous. First, one of the main advantages in skiing is that you are never too old to learn. If you can walk, you can ski. In fact, I know several people who cannot walk, but with the aid of special devices do an admirable job of getting down the mountain. Obviously, if you are a sixty-year-old man, you are not going to win any Olympic gold medals, but you can certainly learn to ski well enough to realize nearly every other benefit of the sport. With rare exception, I cannot think of another sport that I can more heartily recommend to our older citizens. Skiing not only will allow them to gradually get back into good physical condition, but also will provide needed stimulation and diversity in the retirement years and keep them in contact with younger generations —all of which I feel are vital to a long and happy life. One point that I hope I make in this book is that *you* can enjoy the sport of skiing. Unlike a sport like water skiing, where you are out of luck if you do not swim or fancy being towed around by a rope, skiing is enjoyable for a multitude of varied reasons—physical, aesthetic, and cultural. You might be interested to know that in some resorts such as Megeve, as many as 80 per cent of the visitors do not ski, but merely come to participate in the special ambience referred to earlier. On the other hand, in other resorts such as my native Val d'Isere, 95 per cent (and this ratio applies to the townspeople as well) are avid skiers.

As far as the second objection is concerned, I feel that there is nothing more foolish than being afraid of appearing foolish. In other words, the only thing we have to fear is the fear of looking foolish itself. Forgive me, President Roosevelt! For me, some of the best experiences in skiing were in the early stages. I can sympathize with you, however, for upon my "retirement" from amateur skiing, when I took up new sports such as golf and tennis, I wanted to be good right away, and sometimes, in my haste to become proficient, I failed to enjoy the process by which I would achieve that end. We all say, "Next year I will be good and then I'll have fun," but that "next year" never comes. My point, very simply, is this: Whether your personal challenge be learning a stem turn or winning an Olympic gold medal, your enjoyment should come from meeting and conquering that challenge, not from being better than your peers. If you can enjoy yourself learning to make a kick turn, or perfecting your parallel turn, you will be a better person for it.

Is skiing dangerous? Answer: Yes—if you do not approach it properly. Beyond the expense factor, perhaps the greatest deterrent to potential skiers (particularly among older people) is the notion that it is dangerous, that sooner or later you will wind up with a broken leg. This is simply no longer the case. Witness my own town of Val d'Isere, where fifteen years ago you would have about ten broken legs per day and now you have five. This statistic is more impressive when you consider that the number of skiers on the mountain during one day has increased by multiples during that period. The reasons for this increase in safety are multifold:

First, the ability of the average skier has improved through more sophisticated instructional techniques, more knowledgeable skiing media, word-of-mouth, and imitation of better skiers. Moreover, today's skier is more affluent and able to spend more time on the more difficult trails and mountains. Another by-product of this affluence is the fact that parents are now able to start their children skiing at a much younger age.

A second reason for the improved safety of skiing is grounded in the fact that today's runs and trails are much better prepared than they were in the past. Today, on most mountains, bumps and other irregularities are trimmed and the slopes groomed on a daily basis by sophisticated grooming machinery.

The skiers themselves are in better condition as well. There exists a greater awareness among today's skiers of physical conditioning and a greater participation on their part in other sports that also prepare one for skiing. More and more people are becoming aware that just a little bit of exercise prior to the ski season will greatly reduce the chance of injuries.

Perhaps the greatest influence, however, has come from the significant improvement that has taken place over the past two decades in skiing equipment. In my opinion, skiing equipment has improved 2,000 per cent since I started skiing at age three in Val d'Isere. These developments will be discussed in some depth in the next chapter.

We have come a long way since the days of baggy pants, long wooden skis, and "beartrap" bindings. The recent technological developments that have taken place in equipment, the innovations in skiing instructional techniques (for examples the "GLM Method"), and increased awareness of the injury-preventing benefits of physical fitness have all contributed to a steady and significant decrease in the number and severity of injuries resulting from skiing.

Before closing this introductory chapter, I would like to give you an idea of what you might expect in the pages to come. As I said earlier, and will say again before we are through, one of the most pleasurable aspects of skiing is its diversity. Skiing is essentially a sport of situations, more specifically a continuous adaptation on the part of the skier to ever-changing conditions that are an amalgam of several variables, including topography, weather, and the relative ability of the skier.

To date, the sport of skiing has generated a considerable amount of literature, most of which fits within the categories of instruction, biography, technical literature, or the good old adventure story. It seemed to me (and fortunately the good folks at Doubleday agreed) that it was high time that someone wrote a practical guide that will provide the basic fundamentals necessary to prepare one physically, mentally, and technically for the task of coping with and enjoying the infinite varieties of situations posed by this most enjoyable sport.

Some time ago, Arnod Palmer wrote a book called *Situation Golf* in which, rather than taking the traditional instructional approach—as he and so many others had in the past—Arnie told his fellow golfers, in very pragmatic and understandable terms, the strategy he would employ in a wide variety of golfing situations. In the final, and by far the longest section of this book, I have attempted to take this pragmatic approach and indicate those adjustments I make in my basic skiing technique as I encounter different types of slopes and different kinds of skiing conditions. It is said that a photograph can be worth a thousand words, and it was upon this premise that I had my friend and ski photographer, John Russell, spend a week with me, during which he took time-lapse photographs of me skiing in every type of terrain and snow imaginable.

You should be aware, however, that at least half the battle in becoming a solid and confident skier takes place *before* you strap on your skis, and it is with this in mind that I have provided materials that I hope are readable, informative, and yet practical regarding the selection of safe and appropriate equipment and preparing yourself physically and mentally so that you may derive the maximum amount of enjoyment (with the least amount of effort) from your skiing.

It has been my observation that in the case of many books, all new and/or meaningful materials could be condensed into ten well-written pages, and the remainder is merely surplusage to fulfill the word requirements of the publisher. Although I obviously hope that this is not the case with *Situation Skiing*, I do feel that my efforts will have been justified if this book leaves you with one or two solid ideas that will make your skiing more enjoyable. At the very least, I hope that after reading it you will feel that this book was well worth the price of a lift ticket and, perhaps more importantly, the leisure time you will devote to reading it and digesting its contents.

With adequate (though not necessarily expensive) equipment, a reasonable commitment to physical fitness, a proper mental attitude, and an awareness of how to cope with the diverse circumstances that present themselves in skiing, all excuses should fall by the wayside, and your skiing experience should become more enjoyable. For me, skiing is a catharsis, and there is no reason why that should not be true for you as well.

PART I

Preparation Is Half the Battle; or,
A Month of Prevention Is Worth
a Year of Cure

Chapter One

PREPARATION PHASE I: THE BODY

Imagine, if you will, a business executive showing up for an important meeting unshaven, in a tattered suit, and with no more preparation than hastily scribbled notes on the back of a napkin. Imagine also a fireman responding to a call with no protective clothing and no water or chemicals in his fire extinguisher. Imagine a race-car driver about to start the Indianapolis 500 without first checking to see that his engine is properly tuned, that he has enough fuel, etc. Obviously these individuals could not expect, absent some unforeseen power or luck, to achieve any measure of success in their various undertakings.

It is therefore curious to me how people who make exhaustive preparations for their day-to-day occupations can expect to achieve any measure of success in skiing without first preparing themselves for the task at hand. The fact is that in skiing—as in many other fields of endeavor—preparation is at least half the battle. The purpose of this chapter is to illustrate how, with minimum disruption of your schedule, and at minimum expense, you can prepare yourself and your equipment, and in so doing, make your skiing safer, easier, and more enjoyable.

When people ask me (as they often do) to list what I consider to be important prerequisites for a good skier, I place physical fitness at the top. The response, especially in America (although this has improved in recent years), is all too often the following:

"Yes, Jean-Claude, but you're a health nut. What about us normal people who have to spend forty hours a week behind a desk pushing a pencil?" I then explain that for me physical fitness does not mean a herculean effort involving ten-mile daily runs, extensive weight-lifting sessions, subsistence on a diet of vitamin pills and strained carrot juice, but rather a reasonable commitment to health and physical fitness through a program that can very easily be incorporated into the lifestyle of the average person. "Health nut?" To me, a person who cares to put out a little extra effort in order to look, feel, and perform all of his functions better and with less effort exhibits a healthy self-respect and is anything but a "nut." In all fairness, I think that in Europe, and more recently—despite the many available conveniences—in America, people's awareness of health and fitness has changed to the extent that one who would have been considered a "health nut" ten years ago is considered to be well-adjusted, together, and aware by today's standards.

Physical fitness—of the type and magnitude I will describe in this chapter—is important to skiing for two primary reasons: First, it greatly reduces the chances of injury on the slopes, and second, it makes the basic but fundamental skiing maneuvers that we shall later discuss easier—in fact, almost effortless.

One of the chief causes of skiing accidents occurs when the skier dives into the sport without preparing himself properly as far as physical conditioning is concerned. This is particularly true in the case of aggressive skiers who think that they can immediately perform at the level they had reached at the end of the previous season. All too many labor under the misconception that they can "ski themselves into shape" and, in the meantime, compensate for their lack of physical fitness with adjustments to their ski bindings. The fact is that (particularly when you are out of shape) your physical condition changes so rapidly in just one day of skiing that it is simply beyond the power of man or machine to make such subtle adjustments to your bindings, and besides, these devices guard against only one class of injuries. Furthermore, if you have ever tired to ski yourself into shape, you know that this entails more than a few days of stiff muscles, which can take a very large chunk out of your ski trip.

A second (and I feel equally compelling) reason for preparing yourself physically for skiing is that all skiing maneuvers—from the simple wedge up to and including downhill racing—are made considerably easier (and in some cases made possible) by a requisite amount of strength in key parts of your body. In addition to strengthening key muscles and prestretching those muscles, tendons, and ligaments most prone to injury in skiing, a regular (not strenuous) and well-balanced program of exercise will give you the periodic cardiovascular workout so vital to the health of your respiratory and circulatory systems and quite conducive to your general good health and longevity.

Finally, the proper type of fitness program will aid immeasurably in helping you combat the subtle but nevertheless exhausting and debilitating stresses put on each one of us by modern society. In short, it will help you look younger, feel younger, and, if it works for you as it has for me, it will allow you to do a better job in every task you face— mental as well as physical.

But who has the time to get in shape? You do! Through participation in sports other than skiing during the off-season, and the consistent incorporation into your everyday schedule of a very simple exercise routine, you will reach a fitness threshold and thereby minimize the chance of injury and maximize the likelihood of fun on the slopes next season.

General Exercise; or, Do Your Thing, But Do It Right

There seems to be a considerable amount of controversy as to which sport most closely approximates skiing (in terms of muscle tone, muscle group utilization, tempo, etc.) and should therefore be used as a substitute for skiing during the off-season. If forced to make a choice, I would list these sports, in the following order of preference: soccer, jogging (running downhill is the best), cycling, and racquet sports (including handball, which would be the best, since it involves ambidexterity).

Although I have run the gamut of extracurricular sports, the sport from the above list that has become the love of my life (apart from skiing—and my family, of course!) is cycling. During the summer months, I would estimate that I average two hundred miles per week on my bicycle, riding to various scenic points with a group of fellow enthusiasts and participating in weekend races at an intermediate amateur level.

Although this activity is certainly beneficial for my skiing, and my general level of fitness and well-being, this is not my motivation. I cycle because I enjoy it, and that brings me to a point that I feel is very important: What sport should you choose to get into shape (and keep in shape) for skiing? Answer: *Your sport,* provided that it involves most of the parts of the body and provides you with a fair amount of cardiovascular activity, and provided further that you practice it on a regular basis—that is, at least two one-hour sessions per week.

I certainly would not want to take you from tennis and put you into jogging on the theory that the latter might be slightly better for your skiing, because unless you truly enjoyed the substitute activity, the converse would certainly be true. My point, and I cannot emphasize it enough, is that most any sport will be sufficient, provided that you pursue it with vigor and regularity. "What," you ask, "if my sport happens to be skiing?" Then, *mon ami,* I would suggest that you find a second activity that meets the above requirements.

Another point I would like to make is that there are many subtle ways in which you can *and should* work extra cardiovascular activity into your daily routine without noticeably upsetting your schedule. I have one friend, for example, a very successful business executive in New York, who will, whenever possible, use his feet rather than a taxi or the chauffeured limousine readily available to him to travel on errands, to lunch, and to his various business appointments. In addition, when weather permits, this man walks (at a brisk pace) the fifteen-odd blocks he must travel to and from work each day. It must work: Since my friend adopted this do-it-yourself transportation program (less than two years ago—which he supplements with a thirty-minute-per-week exercise program similar to the one set forth in the following pages), he has undergone a rather dramatic transformation, losing more than thirty pounds, redistributing his weight to where nature intended it, and increasing his vigor and vitality in nearly every respect. Another example: A second friend, who (although this is not particularly relevant he is the publisher of one of the largest newsmagazines in the United States) maintains that one of the key elements of his fitness program and a major way in which he gets his legs in shape for the ski season is to hold himself in a position with his knees half bent while he shaves and brushes his teeth each morning. Please don't laugh—it must work —he's quite a skier!

Although this type of adjustment may not necessarily be applicable in your particular situation, I am sure that you can see ways in which minor modifications to your life-style might have the same effect.

No matter what it is, *your sport* should be good for your skiing, provided you pursue it with vigor and regularity. However, you know what they say about too much of a good thing!

At Last, a Reasonable Exercise Routine; or, Ten Minutes a Day the Killy Way

Although the general fitness you will derive from your chosen sporting activity will help greatly to build your strength, endurance, and co-ordination, there are important exercises that, if done on a regular basis, can supplement those activities, at the same time stretching out and elasticizing the muscles, tendons, and ligaments most often injured in skiing mishaps. It is with the realization that most of you have neither the time nor the inclination to adhere to a Spartan exercise program that I have put together a program that should take no more than one hour of your time each week and yet provide you with the minimum you will need to get you to that plateau of fitness I mentioned earlier—a state of fitness that, athough it will not prepare you for the rigors of competition, should enable you to get more enjoyment out of your skiing (particularly during the first few times out) and substantially reduce the likelihood of injury. Now let me ask you the following questions:

- Do you want to substantially reduce the danger of skiing?
- Do you want to improve your ability to ski well under all conditions?
- Do you want to get more enjoyment out of your skiing and, for that matter, life in general?
- Are you willing to pay the price by exerting the extra energy it will take to make these things happen?

If your answer to these questions is "No," then close the book and put it back on the shelf or give it to a friend. If your answer is "Maybe," then read on. If your answer is "Yes," raise your right hand and repeat after me:

I do hereby solemnly swear that henceforth I shall:

- Choose a second sport and practice it on a regular basis during the off-season.
- Put a little extra energy into everything I do—for my skiing.
- Read, absorb, and practice no fewer than three times a week the following exercise routine.

The Killy Routine

It is my recommendation that you practice the following ritual at least three times a week, preferably in the morning before your morning shower and breakfast. Many top sportsmen (and more recently, executives) start their day with such a routine and have discovered that their productivity has increased significantly, since they are in better physical shape (physical and mental health go hand-in-hand) and, moreover, an early-morning workout accelerates the awakening of the bodily processes, adding productive hours to the day and, believe me, working wonders for the disposition.

I have designed this exercise program with you, the civilian skier, not Superman or Wonder Woman, in mind. I have seen hundreds of fitness programs—some voluminous works in themselves—most of which suffer from the same fatal defect: They are written by the purist who would like to see everyone else become purists, and they ignore the fact that the average person does not have the time, energy, inclination, or machinery to follow such a rigorous regimen. The Killy Routine does not require a pretty gym suit, a gymnasium filled with complicated and expensive props and apparatuses; nor does it require mercurial speed, herculean strength, or monastic dedication. It is, I hope, a rather simple routine that *you* should be able to live with and regard not as an unpleasant chore or labor of love, but as an integral and ultimately automatic part of your life-style.

There are two basic rules you must keep in mind if this program is to be effective:

RULE NO. I: You must pursue it with *regularity*. We have made the routine short and simple so that, home or away, rain or shine, there will be *no excuses* for missing an exercise day. For emphasis, and to further illustrate this point, I will provide you with a list of acceptable excuses:

EXCUSE

- Paralysis • Terminal illness • Being kidnaped, bound, and gagged by terrorists • Temporary or permanent diability (for example, body cast)
- Temporary or permanent coma

NOT AN EXCUSE

- Mild illness, (for example, common cold, headache, etc.) • Hangover
- Studying for exams • Traveling • Holidays

RULE No. II: Do each of these exercises exactly as I have described them (that is, with *full* extensions of each movement) and as they are depicted in the accompanying photographs. If you do not, the only person you will cheat will be yourself.

The Killy Routine consists of three stages:

Warmup: Exercises designed to loosen stiff muscles and joints and "warm up" your cardiovascular system to prepare it for the strain of the more strenuous exercises to come, much as you would warm up the engine on your car before driving fast in cold weather.

Workout: Isotonic exercises—to expand the capabilities of your cardiovascular system and, at the same time, build strength and agility.

Stretch and Relax: It is important to know that for each exercise there should be a counterexercise lest you develop an imbalance among the muscle groups. For example, if you did nothing but sit-up exercises, with no counterbalancing exercise for the back, such as the "cobra" position (or back arch), you would have a tendency to overdevelop your abdominal muscles at the expense of your back muscles, which could result in poor posture (that is stooping or slouching) and vulnerability to injury. These stretching and relaxing exercises not only stretch out the muscles you have tightened during your isotonic exercises but also prestress and elasticize the muscles, tendons, and ligaments most often injured in skiing accidents.

Please note that the Killy Routine is intended to be an integral part of your life-style *all year,* not an annual fall crash course to get in shape for the ski season. This includes the winter season as well, and I am confident that you will find the routine, particularly the stretching part, relevant and helpful during skiing vacations; in the morning to stretch out stiff muscles and prepare you for the slopes, and in the evening to stretch out the muscles taut from the day's activities, help you relax, and lessen the likelihood that you will be stiff the following morning.

PHASE ONE: WARMUP

Exercise I: Jogging in Place

Here you want to jog up and down on the balls of your feet, lifting your knees as high as possible. *Note:* These exercises are easier to do if you make them fun. Although I do not need it personally, others have told me that music helps. In fact, if you have a certain dance you like to do that provides all of the exercise of running in place—why not?

Number of repetitions: first week—200 steps in two minutes; second week—300 steps in two minutes; third week and each week thereafter—450 to 500 steps in three minutes.

Exercise II: Neck Rotations
In this exercise the object is to keep your body erect and still with your hands on your hips, rotating your head in a full circle—first in one direction and then the other.

Number of repetitions: Ten circles in each direction. Approximate time: thirty seconds.

Exercise III: Upper-body Rotation

Again, stand erect, with the feet approximately two feet apart and flat on the floor, with your hands placed on your hips. This exercise consists of bending at the waist and rotating your upper body in a full circle—first one way and then the other. In the accompanying photograph, I am in the forward phase of a counterclockwise rotation. Remember that, in this exercise, the hips remain stationary, and it is the *upper body* that rotates. If you perform this and the other rotational exercises in this group properly, you will soon notice that you are able to make wider rotations, and before too long, your body will begin to feel looser and more relaxed.

Number of repetitions: ten in each direction. Approximate time: thirty seconds.

Exercise IV: Hip Rotation

In the same basic position, you now rotate your hips first in one direction and then in the other. Number of repetitions: Ten in each direction. Approximate time: thirty seconds.

PHASE TWO: WORKOUT

Exercise V: The Pushup

The pushup, although one of the oldest and most traditional exercises, remains, in my opinion, one of the best to build strength through the whole body. In doing your pushups, you should remember to keep your body rigid throughout all phases of the exercise. You should be careful not to arch your back in this exercise, since that can be dangerous to your spine. Also note that in a proper pushup, the contraction is done with the arms and shoulders, not with an up-and-down motion of the neck or a bending at the waist.

Repetitions/time: first week—ten in fifteen seconds; second week—fifteen in twenty seconds; third week—twenty in twenty-five seconds, fourth week—thirty in thirty-five seconds; fifth week and each week thereafter—two sets of twenty in twenty-five seconds per set.

Exercise VI: Half Knee Bends

The difference between this exercise and the common "deep knee bend" is subtle but critical. This is an exercise that I learned very recently and that I have found is very effective in building up key skiing muscles in the legs. The important points to remember in this exercise are: First, keep your body erect through the exercise, bending only in the knees and ankles (during the early stages, you will probably want to use a wall for balance, as I am doing in the accompanying photographs). Second, this exercise should be done on the balls of your feet or, even better if you have the strength and agility, your tiptoes. Finally, you should not bend the knee joints much beyond a ninety-degree angle since, in the opinion of many doctors (and the personal experience of some whom I have known), full knee bends can do more harm than good to the cartilage and other tissue of the knees.

Repetitions/time: first week—ten in fifteen seconds; second week—fifteen in twenty seconds; third week—twenty in twenty-five seconds; fourth week and each week thereafter—twenty-five or more repetitions in thirty seconds.

Exercise VII: Stomach Builder 1

This very important exercise is difficult to do at first and becomes increasingly manageable—in fact, easy—after the first two or three weeks. The photographs show the limits of this contraction. From the starting position in photograph above, you simultaneously bring your arms forward and your knees back until they overlap, as in photograph below. It is important in doing this exercise to keep your head up with your chin to your chest and your back flat upon the ground. By doing this, you will focus the torque from the exercise on development of your abdominal muscles, rather than putting unneeded stress on your spine, as is the case with many of the traditional "situp" exercises.

Exercise VIII: Stomach Builder 2

"Stomach builder" is really a misnomer for this exercise, for it contributes not only to the development of the abdominal muscles, but to those of the shoulders, back, hip sockets, and legs as well. This exercise is similar to the previous one in that, for the same reasons stated above, you should attempt to keep your chin to your chest and your back flat on the ground throughout the contraction. As you can see from the photographs, the main difference here is that this exercise involves a crossover in which you touch the inside of your right knee with the inside of your left elbow, and vice versa. This is another exercise that is somewhat difficult at first, but becomes quite easy as you develop the proper muscle groups.

Repetitions/time: first week—ten in fifteen seconds; second week—fifteen in twenty seconds; third week—twenty in twenty-five seconds; fourth week and each week thereafter—twenty-five or more in thirty seconds.

Exercise IX: Skip a Rope

Rope skipping or rope jumping is a time-honored exercise that in my opinion is not only enjoyable, but also one of the best all-around conditioners I can think of; an exercise that is not only a hard to match cardiovascular workout, but also a developer of body co-ordination, strength, speed, agility, and, if practiced enough, endurance. Ah yes, I have now gone against my earlier word and included a piece of apparatus in my exercise routine. My apologies, but you must admit that nothing could be less expensive or easier to carry with you than a simple piece of rope. Skipping rope can, of course, involve a variety of maneuvers such as double jumps, skipping, hopping on one leg at a time, and so on. The benefits you will receive from this exercise are limited only by the energy you put into it.

Repetitions: One minute or more per session.

Exercise X: The Haute Savoie Rope Dance (as opposed to the Mexican hat dance)

I call this the *haute savoie* rope dance because, frankly, I could think of no better name for it. Can you? This exercise has an obvious application to skiing, and is useful to build up the muscles and patterns of co-ordination that you would use in executing that maneuver known as the "short-swing"—that is, a quick series of short-radius, carved parallel turns. Note in the photographs how the upper part of my body stays quiet, relaxed, and facing forward, while my knees and ankles do most of the work to shift me from one position to the next. You might find it interesting to compare my positions in these photographs with my positions in the photographs accompanying the shortswing section of Chapter Seven of this book.

Repetitions/time: first week—ten in fifteen seconds; second week—fifteen in twenty seconds; third week—twenty in twenty-five seconds; fourth week and each week thereafter—twenty-five or more in thirty seconds.

PHASE THREE: STRETCH AND RELAX

Begin this phase by repeating two revolutions (in both directions) of Exercises II, III, and IV; then proceed as follows:

Exercise XI: The Side Stretch

Assume the same basic position as for the previous three exercises (II, III, and IV) and bend the body, first to one side and then to the other, keeping it straight in all other respects.

Repetitions/time: first week—five in each direction in ten seconds; second week—ten in each direction in twenty seconds; third week and each week thereafter—fifteen in each direction in thirty seconds.

Exercise XII: Groin Stretch

This exercise can be invaluable in avoiding injuries to the groin and inner-leg muscles in skiing situations such as that when you happen to catch an inside edge and inadvertently do the "splits." In this exercise you start with your feet spread as wide as possible and facing forward, your hands on your hips, your upper body erect and, as in the accompanying photographs, you shift your weight to the ball of one foot, bending the corresponding knee, at the same time stretching the muscles on the inside of the opposite leg. Once you have stretched as far as you can go—and then some—you repeat the process on the other side.

Number of repetitions: With these stretching exercises, you will soon get a "feel" for when you are stretched out. At the beginning, however, I would recommend five stretches in each direction per session.

Exercise XIII: Achilles Stretch

This exercise was designed to stretch the hamstring, the Achilles tendon, and the muscles in the back of the legs, thereby reducing the likelihood of the injuries to those areas, which so commonly result from forward falls when the bindings do not release properly. This exercise is done from a position similar to the starting position for the push-up and consists of alternately pushing the heels backward to the floor.

Number of repetitions: Ten for each leg per session.

Exercise XIV: The Hurdler Stretch

As you can see from the accompanying photo, I have tucked my right foot behind me and, keeping my left leg extended, am beginning to bend forward over that leg, stretching not only the muscles, tendons, and ligaments in the back of my left leg, but my groin area and the thigh muscles of my right leg as well. Once I have gone forward as far as possible in this position, I repeat this procedure on the other side.

Number of repetitions: Two per side per session.

Exercise XV: The Squat Position

The purpose of this very simple exercise is to carefully stretch out the ligaments of the knees without risking the damage possible from deep knee bends. As you can see from the photo, this exercise consists of standing on your tiptoes, going down as far as you can without doing damage to your knees, and then bouncing up and down very gently on the balls of your feet, thereby stretching out the ligaments and tendons in the knee area.

Number of repetitions: One per session.

Exercise XVI: Heel Sit

This exercise is exactly as it sounds and appears: You sit upright on your heels and bounce lightly up and down, further stretching out the knees, ankles, and the muscles and tendons along the front of your legs. A further extension of this exercise can provide a good counter to the isotonic stomach builders done earlier: From this basic position, you drop your hands to the side, arch your back as far as possible, and then slowly pull yourself back up to the original position.

Exercise XVII: Up and Shake Loose

This is the final exercise of the series, and consists of bouncing up and down on the balls of your feet, alternately relaxing and shaking loose your arms and legs—much in the same fashion as you have seen boxers do before and during prize fights.

Some Words on Diet

Although I certainly do not consider myself (or hold myself out to be) an expert on nutrition, I have over the years made a personal study of the very close relationship between proper nutrition and physical fitness, and (through trial-and-error more than anything else) have evolved a set of rules and values that I have incorporated into my lifestyle and that are now second nature to me.

RULE I: *Don't overeat.*

Eat only what you need to stay healthy and avoid excess whenever possible. I realize that for some people this is very difficult, since for them eating is very much a response to urges, nervous or otherwise, over which they have little or no control. One friend of mine has overcome his propensity to snack between meals by keeping a pitcher of ice water on his desk and taking a drink rather than a bite when these urges strike.

RULE II: *Eat three well-balanced meals each day.*

By well-balanced I mean a diet that contains meats, green vegetables, a reasonable (but not excessive) amount of carbohydrates, fruits, grains, and other foods, such as dairy products, which have a rich store of protein. A note on the relative worth of proteins and carbohydrates: I have read (and this has been confirmed by my personal experience) that although carbohydrate-rich foods (such as the sugars and starches we get from such foods as fruit, potatoes and breads) are normally given credit for being good energy foods, it is the protein-rich foods (such as meats, poultry, fish, nuts, and dairy products) that are the real energy foods which, as they help build new body tissue, provide sustained energy that lasts far beyond the rapid burst one receives from the carbohydrates.

A further argument for proteins is that they tend to be less fattening. In fact, some doctors have theorized that many people who have a weight problem have what amounts to an "allergy" to carbohydrates, and many people have made rather dramatic reductions in their weight with low-carbohydrate diets. It is my feeling, however, that although one should recognize the difference between protein and carbohydrates, and stress the former in their diet, the carbohydrates do, nevertheless, play an important role, providing short-term energy and the bulk and roughage fundamental to a well-balanced diet. In this regard, my favorite carbohydrate-rich foods are whole-grained breads and cereals.

RULE III: *Breakfast like a king, lunch like a prince, and supper like a pauper.*

This old adage, in my opinion, makes a great deal of sense, and I attempt to follow it whenever possible. Without a doubt, breakfast is the most important meal of the day, since it must provide the fuel we need to get full productive use from our body and mind during the most active part of the day. Unfortunately, many people tend to treat breakfast just the opposite, considering a cup of coffee and a roll as adequate fare. It is my feeling that it is extremely important to start the day with an adequate supply of protein in store. If you are one of those who eat little or nothing for breakfast, I suggest that you try starting your day with a breakfast similar to that set forth in the sample diet below, and I am confident that you will soon see that your mornings will become physically and mentally more productive. A typical breakfast at the Killy household:

- One glass of orange juice (or grapefruit half)
- One bowl of high-protein, vitamin-enriched natural cereal with sliced fruit and natural, unflavored yogurt
- One or two soft-boiled eggs
- Milk or coffee

LUNCH

Under the theory to which I ascribe, lunch is the second most important meal of the day and should be a well-balanced combination of meat (or other protein-enriched food), vegetables, and carbohydrates. A typical Killy lunch:

- Steak
- A green vegetable such as broccoli
- Whole-grain bread and/or potatoes
- Milk or table wine and/or mineral water
- Cheese and sliced fruit for dessert

SUPPER

Although dinner is the least important meal as far as nutrition is concerned, it is, nevertheless, an important family ritual in many households, since it is one of the few times during the day when the entire family can spend time together and rehash the day's adventures. There are, however, three things you should consider: First, since the day is nearly over, your protein and carbohydrate requirements are less than they were earlier in the day, and therefore you should avoid eating large quantities during the evening meal. Second, supper should be eaten as early in the evening as possible, so that your body has a chance to digest the food before you go to bed. You should never, I am told, go to bed with a full stomach. A typical Killy supper:

- Green salad
- Broiled chicken
- Spinach
- Potatoes (small portion)
- Yogurt and strawberries for dessert

Many have asked me over the years what kind of foods I eat, and I think that they somehow expect to hear a long list of French and/or health-food exotica. As you can see, my diet is very much like yours; perhaps the only difference is in the quantities, the ratio of protein to carbohydrates, and the timing.

As a late and great friend of mine (a southern promoter of considerable renown) used to say: "My friend, I'm just a simple country boy —a boy from the bush—a meat-and-potatoes man through and through." The message of my diet-related pontification is relatively simple: There is no need to radically change your life-style as long as you approach the table with an attitude of moderation and an appreciation for and reasonable observation of the nutritional guidelines set forth above.

SOME WORDS ON SLEEP

Now that I have taken the liberty of intruding into your personal life and attempted to change your time-honored habits, I might as well give you the Killy philosophy on sleep, an attitude very well captured by that old homily "Early to bed and early to rise makes one healthy, wealthy, and wise."

Seriously, if you spent any time with me, I am afraid you would be disappointed to learn that I am really a very boring fellow. In fact, unless necessity dictates otherwise, it is my usual practice to be in bed around ten o'clock and up by seven for my morning exercise. Of course, this routine must be compromised during the many days I spend away from home on business, frequently traversing several time zones in a single day.

Let me wrap this up before you fall asleep. It is a well-known fact that the individual requirement for sleep varies radically from person to person, and you certainly are the best person to know how much sleep you need each night in order to function to full capacity during the following day. Your watchword, however, should be *consistency*. Once you find how much sleep you need, you should try to maintain that level every day—harmonized, of course, with the compromises you must make in accordance with your various priorities. For me, eight hours a day is one of my top priorities. But, of course, I'm a health nut.

Chapter Two

PREPARATION PHASE II: EQUIPMENT, SELECTION, AND MAINTENANCE

Since my early days, there has been an evolution in the sophistication of skiing equipment that has produced several significant changes that make skiing not only much safer, but much easier and enjoyable as well.

Naturally, these changes are meaningless unless you are aware of them. The purpose of this chapter is to provide you with an easy-to-read survey of the most important of these innovations. In the same manner as I tried to avoid being overly demanding regarding physical fitness, I will try to avoid being overly technical on the subject of equipment, yet provide you with some basic hints regarding its selection and maintenance and some meaningful information regarding recent innovations in equipment and accessories that, I hope, will help you get more out of your skiing.

THE BOOT

In my opinion, there is no piece of equipment that contributes more to one's ability to ski well than the ski boot. When I started skiing, ski boots were little more than heavy leather shoes that provided less support than do most of today's hiking shoes. Today's boots are made of strong, resilient, but lightweight plastic and are fastened shut by a variety of easy-to-use buckle systems, most of which have a fair degree of adjustment factor. These higher and firmer boots of today provide firmer (particularly lateral) support, which helps you avoid twisted ankles at some, but not all, angles and does a great deal of the work involved in transmitting the energy from your body to the skis.

A good ski boot will provide this firm lateral support and yet allow for enough forward flexibility so that you do not bruise your shins and so that you retain the requisite degree of flexibility in your knees and ankles. For a period of time during the early seventies, there was a technological overreaction among ski boot manufacturers to the "bedroom slipper" boots of yesteryear, which resulted in a generation of boots that were too high and rigid; the unfortunate result was that these monsters tended to lock the skier into a forward position that all but eliminated the flexibility of the knee and ankle which, at least in my opinion, is a vital prerequisite to good skiing. These boots were also quite uncomfortable, and due to their forward inflexibility, have been blamed for causing a number of boottop injuries to the bones of the lower leg.

Over the past couple of years, we have witnessed a needed and refreshing retreat from these excesses. With the technology and the quality of materials used in ski boot manufacture constantly improving, we have learned that a shorter, and in some respects softer, boot can now do the job—with considerably more ease and comfort to the skier. When asked which brand of boot I recommend, I reply that although I am partial to the French made Le Trappeur, and have used it and contributed to its development over the years, there are four or five boots now on the market that are roughly comparable in quality. As for construction, I prefer the front-entry buckle-type hinged boot.

There are, however, several important things you should keep in mind when selecting a ski boot:

- Select a boot that is compatible with the contour of your foot. All of the different brands of boots have slightly different contours, and no two feet are alike; so I would suggest that you try each of the major brands to see which one fits you best.
- Make sure that you get a proper fit. Many people have a tendency to buy boots that are too large and then try and compensate with many

layers of stockings. This is no good. Unless you have a firm-fitting yet comfortable boot, there is no way that you will be able to have the subtle control over your skis necessary for good skiing. I personally wear a thin street-sock and light wool sock beneath my boots and buy my boots just long enough so that, when the boot is completely buckled, there is a small amount of space (e.g., ¼ inch) between the front of the boot and my longest toe. Most of today's better ski shops are fully versed in fitting the various types and brands of boots, and you should feel free to spend the necessary time with your authorized dealer to get a proper fit. Believe me, a proper-fitting boot can make the difference between agony and ecstasy, and a couple of extra minutes invested in the selection process will be well worth it once you hit the slopes!

- Make sure you buy a boot that is warm. Your dealer should be able to help you in this regard.
- When buying ski boots, don't be "penny wise and pound foolish." If the shoe fits, wear it! Even though you may have to spend a few extra dollars, it will be well worth it—those extra dollars will come back many times over in terms of increased skiing enjoyment.

THE SKI

Today's skis are designed to carve, turn, and maneuver more easily than before, thereby saving you energy. Without a doubt, the greatest innovation in the evolution of skis has been the coming of the plastic age. During the late 1960s, I had the pleasure of participating at first hand (along with my fellow members on the French team, including my friend and associate Michel Arpin) in the development of the Fiberglas ski. Through a great deal of experimentation, we learned that a glass-wrapped (as opposed to sandwich-type) Fiberglas ski was not only stronger (and safer—no broken ski tips to watch out for) than the traditional wood and metal skis, but also possessed a flexibility and resilience that put previously impossible maneuvers well within the reach of the average advanced skier. These skis not only carved a better turn, but also, if properly utilized, possessed the ability to rebound, accelerating the skier out of one turn and into the next. It was this acceleration that formed the basis for what the media referred to in the middle and late sixties as my "brink-of-disaster technique." Where observers surmised that I was purposely thrusting my skis out in front of me, I was, in reality, fighting to keep up with these remarkable new skis.

Concurrent with the development of the modern Fiberglas skis, we began to learn more and more about the concept of side camber. If you have not noticed, a ski is generally wider toward the tips and tails than it is at the center. If you lay your skis flat on the ground and place them side by side with the tips and the tails in contact, you will note that there is a space between the inside edges of the two skis that is widest toward their center. It is this inward curvature of the side walls and edges of the skis that is referred to as side camber, and it is this property that makes it possible to carve, rather than slide, the skis in an arc while making a turn. The greater the side camber relative to the length of the ski, the shorter the turning radius of the ski. Therefore, a downhill ski generally has less side camber than a giant slalom ski, and a giant slalom ski less side camber than a slalom ski. Some skis (less common today than a few years ago) will have more side camber on one side than the other. This can be determined by placing the sides together, their bottoms on the floor as described above, measuring the widest point between the inside edges of the two skis, and then reversing the position of the skis and measuring the widest point between the two opposite edges. If there is in fact a difference, the bindings should be mounted so that the widest space is between the *inside* edges of the skis.

You should be aware that the location of this widest point varies from brand to brand (and even pair to pair), and it is the location of this point that determines the point from which the skis can be most easily turned—that is, if the wide point is farther back, the ski will tend to turn easier when the weight is farther back on the ski, and, of course, the converse is true.

It is no mystery that in addition to variations in length and amount of side camber, skis have varying degrees and patterns of flex. For example, some may be easier to bend than others, some may be stiffer in the tips than at the tails, while some may have a fairly even flex throughout. How then does one battle through this jungle of esoterica and determine which pair is most appropriate in his particular case?

Some practical advice: Although you obviously need a specialized ski in a specialized situation—for example, ballet skis for freestyle ballet competition, downhill skis for downhill racing, etc.—the type of ski I prefer (and recommend to you) for a wide variety of recreational skiing is one that is easy to turn and is adaptable to a wide range of skiing situations, one that has a medium degree of side camber, turning point at or near the center, and a soft, even flex pattern. Although quality control at the major ski manufacturers is improving year by year, you still occasionally run into a situation where a pair of skis are not particularly well matched. This is undesirable, since it is very important that your skis react alike. A knowledgeable and competent dealer should be able to help you pick out a pair of skis that have the qualities I have described above. If not, or if there is a limited selection, I recommend that you shop around—it will be well worth your time in the long run.

Another major innovation of modern ski technology, and one that has been with us since the early 1960s, is the polyurethane base, most commonly referred to by such trade names as "Kofix" and "P-tex." These bases are not only faster, but also perform with more consistency over a wide degree of temperature and snow conditions. This, of course, contributes greatly to the safety and enjoyment of your skiing, since it allows you significantly more control over your skis.

Ski edges have improved greatly as well. Today's thinner and easier-to-maintain edges do a great deal of the carving, gripping, and holding for the skier, since the tempered steel of which today's edges are made provides a much more tenacious and consistent bite on the snow and ice than did the old, wider, screw-in type, which were too soft in some conditions, too hard in others and, because of their width and uneven nature, would often grab and sometimes catch in the snow, contributing to many an undeserved spill and the time-honored cliché "I guess I caught an edge."

Although it may not be obvious that the skis of today are much safer than the skis of fifteen years past, it is absolutely true.

Long Ski or Short Ski—That Is the Question

The development of the short or compact ski has undoubtedly been a major ski-related innovation of the seventies. The short ski has made a significant contribution to our sport in two major ways. First, although I am not a physicist, it seems logical that a shorter ski can produce less resistance in the snow and exert considerably less leverage and torque than a longer one and, from what I am able to determine, this decreased torque has resulted in a rather significant reduction in the per capita number of lower leg injuries. The second benefit lies in the fact that short skis are much easier for the skier to turn, resulting in a lessening of fatigue and resultant injuries to veteran skiers and making skiing a much easier and quicker sport to learn for the novice. It also enables the average skier to become more proficient and handle a far wider variety of conditions than was previously possible on the old boards.

These short or compact skis of which I speak are not shorter models of the traditional alpine recreational ski, but specialized skis which, although shorter (typical sizes are 170 and 180 centimeters), are wider than the conventional ski. These dimensions provide the necessary surface area to support a larger skier but, since there is obviously much less resistance in a 180-centimeter board than a 210-centimeter board, they make the modern compact ski much easier to turn.

The short ski era has not been all positive, however, and although I would recommend them to the beginner and to the intermediate skier who skis once or twice a year, the compact ski is by no means an appropriate tool for the expert recreational skier. The reason for this is that they are not stable at high speeds (evidence has shown that upper-body injuries have increased for that reason). Furthermore, short skis have enabled less proficient skiers to ski at their own pace on more advanced slopes, carving out short, choppy moguls that are incompatible with the technique, speed, and equipment of expert skiers on longer skis, leading to frustration and even injury to that group. Like most good things, the compact ski has been oversold, and believe me, this has almost ruined the sport of skiing for some of us old-timers who now find our favorite runs almost impossible to ski unless they have been groomed that very day. It is my recommendation (and I know that this has been implemented at some areas) that special areas—that is, the expert runs—be set aside for those who use the longer skis. It is also my feeling that there are a great number of skiers who simply have no business on short skis and who, perhaps as an over-reaction to the excess length and difficult turning properties of the skis of yesteryear, have jumped from a 207-centimeter or longer ski to a

Short ski or long ski? The choice is yours.

170 or 180, whereas a 195 or 200 would be more appropriate under most circumstances. I feel that 195 centimeters is a good length for the average advanced recreational male skier, while 180 centimeters is the appropriate length for the average advanced female recreational skier. Since ski length is dictated not only by one's height, but also by such factors as weight, strength, skiing experience, and overall athletic ability, this will vary from case to case. A competent specialty ski shop will be well versed in this matter, and I recommend that you seek their consultation in this regard. There is, however, one area where the dubious propriety of compact skis for expert skiers does not apply: deep-powder skiing. Although I normally ski on a 203–205-centimeter ski, I have found my 180-centimeter K-2 shorts absolutely delightful, and in fact preferable to longer skis, in skiing the deep powder.

It is my feeling that what we really need to develop for the competent recreational skier is a high-performance compact ski—a ski that combines the positive aspects of today's compact skis with certain distinguishing characteristics, such as the extra dampening and side camber, of the longer high-performance skis. These "supercompacts" should be in two lengths: 195 centimeters for men and 180 centimeters for women. In fact, I am presently working with my associates at K-2 on introducing a new "midline" that will employ these very characteristics.

The Safety Binding

Although its advent came unheralded by marching bands, sky rockets, or front-page headlines, the development of the safety binding has to be the greatest contribution to our sport since man first found that he could more easily traverse the great snows by strapping boards to his feet. Prior to the introduction of the modern safety binding, we used what were known as beartrap bindings. Beartraps they were! So firmly did those gadgets affix your foot to the ski that you might as well have been nailed to the ski itself. Needless to say, with the long old-fashioned wooden skis, the soft low-cut boots, and the beartrap bindings, skiing was indeed a daredevil enterprise for the young and lion-hearted. That, as we have seen, is no longer the case.

Since their introduction in the late 1950s, safety bindings have undergone a subtle but steady evolution—to the point that the development and manufacture of safety ski bindings has become an industry unto itself and a fertile academic discipline for engineers and orthopedic doctors as well. The ever-increasing mass of literature on the subject of binding adjustment is ample evidence of the complexity of this area; so complex, in fact, is the technical jargon of binding selection and adjustment that I shall defer to the experts and attempt only to provide you with a crash course (no pun intended) on the subject, based on my own limited knowledge.

Although I have one favorite brand of binding (Look Nevada), which I have used for years, there are several good bindings on the market that if properly adjusted and maintained, will provide you with a safe release from your skis at that critical moment. Although I personally prefer step-in-type bindings, it seems to me that the modern plate bindings may be the best way to go for the average skier, since they release in nearly every direction.

In selecting your ski bindings, make sure that you go to a knowledgeable dealer and give him all relevant information regarding you and your skiing ability, particularly your height, weight, strengths and weaknesses, age, physical condition, skiing, and overall athletic ability. From this input, he should be able to make a good recommendation as to which type and brand of binding are most appropriate for you as well as how your bindings should be mounted and adjusted.

Never allow your bindings to be mounted on your skis or adjusted by anyone other than an authorized dealer for that type of binding. In this connection, it is of critical importance that your bindings are at all times properly adjusted and that the adjustment is based on *current* input. There are three basic methods of adjusting bindings:

- *Bench Test:* Here you stand on a bench, fastened to your skis, and attempt to cause your bindings to release by exerting pressure in various directions while an expert makes appropriate adjustments.
- *Adjustment by Machine:* In this procedure, the dealer consults a chart indicating what your particular release coefficients should be and then adjusts the bindings to those specifications through the use of a special pressure-sensitive machine.
- *Trial and Error:* This is the method where you learn by injuring a

limb because your binding does not release when it should, or perhaps releases prematurely, causing an unexpected fall. Frankly, I prefer the first two methods above.

The problem with both of the first two methods above, however, is that it is very difficult to duplicate on-snow conditions in a shop, since many other variables such as water, snow, and great variations in temperature may intervene. The advantage of the machine-test method is that it is based on scientific information, and the machine tests not only the skier's ability to release the binding, but also tests the binding itself and measures it against sets of standards set forth by the various binding manufacturers. Although these methods of binding adjustment do not provide a panacea, they certainly beat the alternative. Although the first adjustment generally works, you should not be afraid to go into the shop every night if that's what it takes to get them right. Further, since your skiing strength will increase over the course of a week (and, for that matter, the season), you may find it necessary to go in for periodic adjustment. Fortunately, many of the modern bindings (especially those of the past couple of years) have increased elasticity, helping you avoid the inconvenience of constant binding adjustment.

Some additional pointers:

- Too loose can be as bad as too tight. Some of my worst mishaps have occurred when my bindings released unexpectedly at a critical moment.
- You should never mix bindings, since manufacturers design all of their components to work together, not with parts of other manufacturers' bindings.
- You should make sure that your boot has been modified to work compatibly with your bindings.
- You should keep your boots and bindings clean and free from water and ice.
- You should keep your bindings lubricated with silicone spray or a similar lubricant that is not influenced by changes in temperature.
- In the case of nonplate bindings, your bindings should be accompanied by a compatible effective antifriction device—a Teflon-coated pad or roller-type device that helps your binding do its job by increasing the predictability and uniformity of release. Many of to-

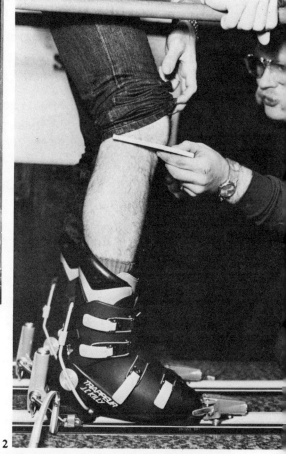

Two methods of binding adjustment:
the bench test and the machine method.

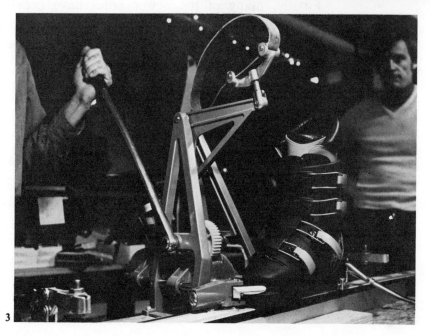

day's better bindings come equipped with such a device. If you add an antifriction device to an existing set of bindings, you should keep in mind that you have introduced a new variable and that your bindings should be adjusted accordingly. Further, your AFDs should be periodically inspected and replaced if worn.

One final note: There are constant improvements being made in this ever-changing field, which are very well covered by leading ski publications such as *Ski* and *Skiing,* and you will be well advised to keep abreast of them. Again, don't be penny wise and pound foolish by skimping in this vital area.

THE POLE

Is it true, as they say, that a pole is a pole is a pole? Perhaps, but there have been some recent developments of which I would like to make you aware. First, poles have become much lighter in recent years, making them easier to use and therefore less tiring. Second, many poles, especially those at the higher end of the various lines, have ice tips that prevent your pole plant from slipping when you are skiing on ice or very hard snow. This can be quite valuable when descending a steep, icy *piste*—a situation where surefootedness and strong, positive pole plants are all-important.

Finally, many of the newer poles have breakaway wrist straps and/or knuckle-protecting plastic grips, both of which I consider to be significant innovations as far as safety is concerned, since they help eliminate hand and wrist injuries.

SKI BRAKES AND SAFETY STRAPS

This should be an important section if you have regard for the safety of others. Although I have worn safety straps since they were introduced (I feel no one has the right to endanger another with a runaway ski), I must admit that they have always made me a bit nervous. When you come out of your bindings in a high-speed fall, but are still connected to your skis by a safety strap, the skis have a tendency to

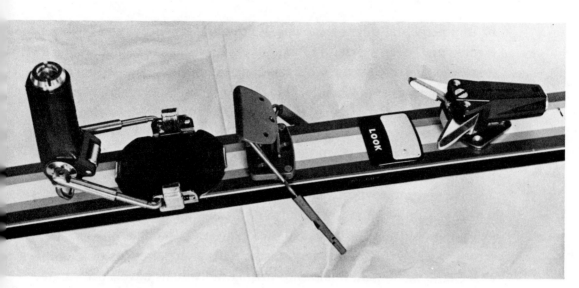

A ski brake in action.

"windmill"—to bounce and whirl around in an unpredictable fashion, with the danger of striking you and causing serious injury. It is for this reason that I prefer the newer, so-called ski brake device, a mechanism that springs open as the bindings are released, projecting an anchor or drag from the ski bottom that soon brings the runaway ski to a halt, hopefully before it can cause injury to another.

CANTING — THE SECRET WEAPON

Ideally, when a person stands on his skis, the bottoms of those skis should be flat to the ground, and he should be exerting no pressure on either the inside or outside edges of either ski. From this position, it will take a minimum amount of lateral movement of the knees and ankles to shift from one edge to another. Unfortunately, nobody is perfect, and most or us are, in varying degrees, knock-kneed or bowlegged, and there must be some type of adjustment between the top surface of our skis and the soles of our boots if we are to ride a flat ski while standing in our natural position. Without such an adjustment, a knock-kneed person would tend to ride too much on the inside edges and, without an awkward outside correction with the knees, would tend to be in a perpetual stem or snowplow position. This results in inefficient turning and, even worse, a crossing of the ski tips at higher speeds. A bowlegged person, on the other hand, has a tendency to ride the outside edges of the skis and, when turning, has to make an exaggerated inward movement with the knee of the outside or downhill ski, often to the point that skiers with this problem tend to tuck that knee behind the other in order to get the proper edge. During my earlier racing days, particularly my early years on the French team, I had plenty of time to analyze and improvise to correct these types of problems, and it was during this period that my friends and I came up with the idea of compensating for these anatomical differences by nailing one or more pieces of leather thong to the inside or outside upper edges of our skis, as the case warranted. Some enterprising individuals have since capitalized on this concept and have developed what are commonly called cants, which are widely available through ski shops to remedy such problems at a very low cost.

There are three methods of determining the amount of canting you will need: the field method (trial and error), the visual method, and the machine method. I prefer the last. Once you have determined the requisite degree of cant, there are three methods of canting:

- By attaching wedge-shaped nylon or plastic plates to the bottoms of your ski boots.
- By placing special commercially produced plastic or nylon wedges between your bindings and skis.
- By grinding the bottoms of your ski boots to the appropriate angles.

Although it has the disadvantage of removing most if not all the traction treads from the bottoms of your ski boots, I prefer the third method since it is lighter, cleaner, and gives you the ability to switch freely among different pairs of skis. Keep in mind, however, that whatever method you choose, you are making a significant alteration to the boot/binding/ski relationship, and you should have your bindings adjusted accordingly. If you have not yet adopted this now not-so-secret weapon, I suggest that you do so as soon as possible. Although it will take some adjustment in your skiing at first, I am confident that you will be pleased with the ultimate results.

2

3

CANTING: THE SECRET WEAPON
A canting machine (photo 1) is the best way to determine the amount of adjustment needed between the boot and the ski (photo 2), and grinding your skis. On this machine, an alignment of the center slots and the centers of the kneecaps would indicate proper canting. Two primary methods of compensation: inserting a wedge-shaped cant between the boot and the ski (photo 2), and grinding the boot soles to the proper angle (photo 3).

On Clothing

Ski clothing has also undergone a steady evolution that, most recently, has been influenced by considerations of safety and practicality. Earlier ski clothes had that "baggy look" which, although fashionable during the era, was downright dangerous, since the clothes could be easily caught in the machinery of the ski lift. During the sixties, ski clothing became increasingly slick, streamlined—and restrictive! Today's ski clothing is tight, but has been made more flexible through the inclusion of expansion gussets and utilization of better stretch fabrics.

One unfortunate characteristic of the slick new look in ski fashions, particularly that billed as the "wet look," was that once you fell on ice or hard snow, particularly on a steep slope, there was very little (absent a tree, another skier, or the bottom of the hill) to impede your descent. In fact, I sometimes wondered whether these "wet look" fabrics would not be better placed on the bottom of downhill skis. Fortunately, the ski apparel industry has reacted in a positive and responsible manner to this problem by developing "antigliss" fabrics with a higher (and safer) coefficient of friction than their sleek but potentially disastrous predecessors.

On Glasses and Goggles

Here is another area where a couple of extra dollars spent can mean the difference between pleasure and pain. The basic requirements:

- For obvious reasons, hardened, shatterproof lenses.
- To eliminate distortion, and provide better protection against ultraviolet rays: surfaced (surfaces parallel) lenses.
- A frame that covers as much of the eye area as possible and is not made of a material that will cut you up if you take a bad spill.

I personally prefer the "photosun"-type sunglasses, which adjust their darkness to suit different lighting conditions. When you buy goggles, make sure they are comfortable, large enough to protect against cold, wind, and sun, and have lenses that are bright enough so that they enable you to see better in fog. The newer antifog goggles are a welcome development and are naturally preferable, although not crucial.

On Gloves

Your gloves should be warm, but not too tight. If they are too tight, you can't grip your poles, and if you can't grip your poles, you may have problems with your balance, and if you have problems with your balance, you may fall and get hurt. Silly—but just another way of saying that even the most seemingly trivial accessories can have much to do with your skiing safety and enjoyment.

Ski Preparation and Maintenance

Unfortunately, many skiers have the misconception that once the bindings have been mounted, the skis are all set, and there is nothing left but to strap them on and go. The truth of the matter, however, is that proper preparation and periodic maintenance of the bottoms of your skis and your edges are every bit as important as buying the right equipment in the first place. There is simply no sense in having the great equipment unless that equipment is properly tuned. If you do not take a little extra time to keep a good pair of skis in proper condition, they will soon lose those properties that made them good skis to begin with.

Although you certainly have the option to have your skis repaired and tuned by a ski mechanic, I will nevertheless give you a short course on the Killy Method in the event that you, like me, prefer to do it yourself. Strange as it may sound, I actually enjoy working on my skis. For me, the responsibility and pride involved in properly caring for my equipment is a very significant part of what skiing is all about. With ski equipment costing what it does today, this philosophy also makes great economic sense. A few minutes of time invested after each skiing session will add months to the useful life of your equipment. Last but not least, it will make your skiing easier, safer, and more enjoyable.

THE KILLY TUNE-UP

Step I: Take a small penknife (or the edge of your scraper) and trim excess damaged base material from the scratches or holes in your ski bottoms.

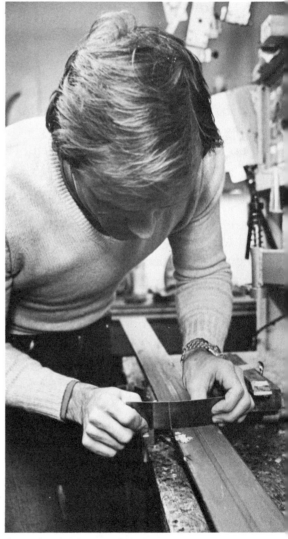

Step II: Light Kofix candle and let burn until melted Kofix is running freely, then drip molten material into damaged areas of ski bottoms. If scratches are deep, fill by making several passes with candle, leaving time for the deposited material to cool rather than attempting to fill all at once. Be very careful with this molten material, for it can start fires and cause serious burns.

Step III: Trim excess material from repaired areas with edge of scraper and scrape ski bottoms with even application of scraper edge until surface is smooth.

Step IV: Flat-file the ski bottoms until flat and smooth, and make sure that the edges and base are on the same plane. The direction of your file strokes should be from tip to tail, and the file should be held at the proper angle (approximately forty-five degrees from the direction of the ski) so that file teeth are biting in the direction of each stroke. Special care should be taken to keep the file flat. If you press down too hard on the ends of the file, you will make your ski bottoms convex, and if you press too hard toward the middle, you will make the bottoms concave; both are undesirable.

Step V: Starting at the tip and working toward the tail, file the sides of the edges, keeping your file pointed in the same direction of the ski edge, and stroke. When side filing, you should strive to hold the file at the appropriate angle so that you hone a perfect ninety-degree edge on your ski. Once you have finished this procedure, it is a good idea to run the file once lightly down the bottom of the skis (in the fashion described in Step IV above) in order to take off any burrs that may have developed during the side filing.

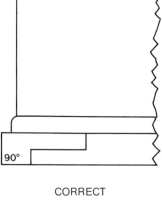

CORRECT

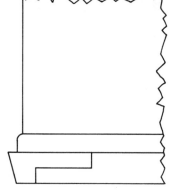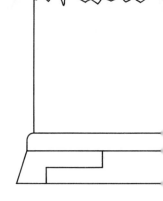

INCORRECT

Step VI: With vigorous strokes, rub wax on ski bottoms, covering them with a thin coating of wax. Obviously there are more sophisticated methods of waxing skis (for example, ironing or painting and scraping—all of which can be done by your specialty ski shop), but I promised to show you just the basics, and frankly, I feel that this procedure is all that is really necessary for noncompetitive skiing situations for most skiers, myself included.

Step VII: Using moderate pressure and vigorous strokes, polish bottoms with a waxing cork. If you do not have a cork handy, a folded newspaper, a piece of cloth, or even the palm of your hand will work quite well.

The Killy Tune-up

Tools:

- 3 × 5 (approximate) tempered steel scraper
- Kofix candles and matches (or, if you prefer, polyethylene base repair material and a soldering iron or similar appliance)
- Medium-size second cut mill or "mill bastard" file
- File card (a brush-type tool with steel bristles to clean your file)
- Appropriate ski wax
- Cork

THE FINAL STEP: WARM UP BEFORE YOU CUT LOOSE

Yes, I've had you in the gym, I've had you in the shop, and now, believe it or not, it is time to make some turns—almost. There is one more little ritual I strongly recommend you endure before pointing them downhill: a "pregame warmup," if you will, that will wake your body and prepare your muscles for what's to come, greatly reducing your chances of injury and enhancing your enjoyment during the first runs of the day. Many skiers, although eager to attack the mountain for a day of skiing, rightly approach their first couple of runs with a certain degree of apprehension. It is colder in the mornings, and it takes several runs before they really get with it. Doesn't it seem ridiculous to waste a good portion of the day (when the snow is untrammeled and the slopes relatively free of skiers) when a more effective warmup could be obtained through a quick and painless exercise session before the first run? I will show you what I do and leave the decision up to you.

I have found this simple exercise routine not only an excellent way to get off to a quick and safe start in the mornings, but I also occasionally use abbreviated versions of it (for example, one or two repetitions of exercises Nos. I, II, III, IV, and VII to limber up and stimulate circulation after lunch or a long ride on a cold chair lift.

WARM UP BEFORE YOU CUT LOOSE, or: KILLY'S LUCKY SEVEN

Warmup No. I: Cross-arm Stretch
This exercise consists of raising the arms to the side, even with the shoulders, and then alternately stretching them back as far as they will go and bringing them together to the point that they are crossing and the elbows are even with one another.
Number of repetitions: ten, alternating which arm is on top during the crossed-arm phase.

Warmup No. II: Upper-body Twist
Here you stand erect, facing forward, with your hands on your hips, and twist your upper torso as far as it will go, first in one direction and then the other, keeping your hips and head facing forward, at the same time striving to bring the shoulders into a position perpendicular to that of the lower body. Number of repetitions: Ten in each direction.

Warmup No. III: Knee Raiser
Standing erect and facing forward, lift one knee and then the other as high as possible, keeping the skis pointed forward, their bottoms parallel to the ground.
Number of repetitions: Five for each leg.

Warmup No. IV: Knee Rotation

Standing erect with poles planted in the snow and feet together, simultaneously rotate both knees in circles as wide as possible, first in one direction and then in the other.

Number of rotations: Five in each direction.

Warmup No. V: Sky-to-skis Body Stretcher

Start from a position standing erect with arms reaching straight up as high as possible, then bend forward at the waist (do not bend the knees) and touch the tops of your skis with your fingertips and, as you become more limber, the palms of your hands.

Number of repetitions: Five (ten if you feel energetic).

Warmup No. VI: Head-to-knee Leg Stretcher

Standing erect with poles planted in the snow, lift one leg out in front of you and plant the tail of the ski in the snow far enough in front of you so that the ski will form a ninety-degree angle with the snow. From this position, bend forward, bringing your forehead as close to the upraised knee as possible.

Number of repetitions: Five on each side.

Warmup No. VII: Achilles Stretcher

Start from an erect position with the poles planted slightly in front of you; slide first one ski and then the other as far as you can straight back, so that you stretch out your Achilles tendon and the muscles in the back of your legs.

Number of repetitions: Five on each side.

A FINAL CHECK LIST
Proper sunglasses, sun screen for exposed areas, safety straps, and a sense of direction will all make your days safer and more enjoyable.

PART II

The Mental Elements
of Good Skiing

Chapter Three

THE FIRST ELEMENT: PROPER INPUT

THE MIND AS A COMPUTER

With all of our great technological achievements, we have yet to come close to duplicating that most sophisticated of all mechanisms: the human brain. Scientists have discovered that our brain functions very similarly to an ultrasophisticated computer with an infinitesimal number of compartments and a storage capacity so vast that we can hope to program only a portion of it during our brief stay on this planet. As I understand it, our brain takes bits of knowledge and stores them in such a way that although they may seem long forgotten, they will, given the proper stimulus, surface, often when you least expect them. This retrieval process seems to be governed by subconscious forces. I am sure that you too have had experiences when all the money in the world could not cause you to recall a fact with which you were conversant days or months before. Then, when the pressure is off and you're relaxed and thinking of something else, presto! Back it comes. I see this as evidence that our computer functions better when the pressure is off and it is left to its own devices, unobstructed by the threats of a failure-fearing ego.

How does this relate to skiing? Well, like bits of information, patterns of physical behavior can be programmed into your computer as well and, as we shall discuss later, are retrieved more easily if they have been subject to repetition and are allowed to occur naturally, unimpeded by conscious thought and fear of failure. However, no matter how sophisticated our computers are, the results will be good only to the extent of the input received. Therefore, the quality of the input and the way in which it is received become quite important.

It is said that a picture is worth a thousand words, and I feel that this maxim rings particularly true when applied to the learning of a physical activity, particularly a complex physical activity such as skiing. It has been my personal experience that images, not words, are the most effective data with which to program your computer for good skiing. By images I do not mean a frozen frame of a skier in a particular pose, but rather the *Gestalt*—the totality of that activity we call skiing. It has been my repeated observation that the best and fastest way to learn a sport is to watch and imitate a champion. When I learned to ski it was not by reading a how-to instructional book and spending hours thinking about how much weight should be on my downhill ski, but rather by skiing behind and imitating the better skiers. They say that there is a great advantage in learning young. Perhaps, but sometimes I think that this is due to the fact that the young do not have a tendency to be over-analytical; when they watch and copy an activity, they absorb the totality of the activity, trusting their computer to break the image down into appropriate commands to the various parts of the body involved in carrying it out successfully. Learning by imitating also involves a certain amount of role playing. In this regard, I don't mind saying that I spent many days as a variety of now-forgotten skiing champions before I became Jean-Claude Killy.

Unfortunately, very few of us are able to ski with the champions (or, for that matter, superior skiers), and that is where the value of such visual aids as skiing movies and stop-action photography come into play.

The Value of Instruction

As I indicated earlier, one of the greatest joys of skiing is the factor of independence—the individual skier's freedom to break away and do his thing when and where he wants. However, before this can happen, one must be competent at least in the basics.

Next to literally following in the ski tracks of the champions, the best way to learn is from a competent instructor (many of whom are champions in their own right), not from a well-meaning friend or relative from whom you can acquire bad habits that may take a lifetime to erase. By listening to and imitating these self-styled experts, you may "improve" fast, but take my word, you are headed down a one-way street that ends short of your goal: becoming an expert skier—one who, although not necessarily flashy, can ski competently under all types of conditions and in every conceivable situation. By exposing yourself to a high caliber of skiing you are, in effect, programming your computer with valuable input, which will serve as a significant shortcut, since it would take years to learn what you are viewing through trial and error. Modern ski instruction is geared with this in mind. Today there is an emphasis on function rather than form and a realization that with a firm grasp on the basics, even the novice can handle most conditions. One theme that has been widely present in skiing instruction since the late sixties is the concept of "wide tracking"—skiing with the skis wider apart for more stability. Although ski writers have tried very hard to make me the father of this, I simply will not take credit, since I do not feel that it is a technique per se, but rather a common-sense application of the basic laws of physics, a way of staying on your feet on steep and icy slopes and a way of accelerating in a turn—but only under specific circumstances. I have said that skiing is not a static picture-book activity but rather a series of adjustments to varying circumstances. For me, this new "technique" came hand-in-hand with the new Fiberglas skis which, due to their lightness, responsiveness, and manueverability, allowed more independence between the two legs. This utilitarian revolution has swept the world of skiing instruction, and today (with the exception of very minor stylistic nuances) this common-sense application of physical principles and better communication among national instructional bodies through the vehicle of Interski have resulted in an international codification of teaching technique with a remarkably uniform end product.

The ski instructors have not only improved and simplified skiing technique, but also they have developed innovative shortcuts that greatly reduce the time it takes for one to become a competent skier. A case in point: the Graduated-length Method of teaching which, although nearly a decade old, is still worth mentioning, since it is a quicker, safer, and more comfortable way to learn to ski, one that enables the average person to become mobile on skis much faster than previously possible through the traditional avenues of instruction. GLM involves four basic steps: a dry-land phase without skis, during which one learns the body physics used to execute basic skiing maneuvers; a short ski phase, in which the skier begins immediately to ski parallel on very short, almost skatelike skis; the intermediate stage, where one gets to a longer (but still short by normal recreational standards) ski, picking up the pace a bit and beginning the first carved turns; and the final graduation to a conventional-length ski, which allows for more stability and cleaner turns at higher speeds.

I have mentioned the importance of receiving proper input through reading, watching, and imitating. However, correct input does not necessarily guarantee proper execution. We all, from time to time, have suffered that perplexing and frustrating experience where, even though we are sure that we are doing everything right, it simply just isn't happening. The reason for this is simple: It is very difficult for you to be aware of your body movements in a dynamic activity like skiing —what you feel may not necessarily be what is. This brings to mind an obvious but often overlooked value of skiing instruction, one particularly relevant to the self-taught skier: an *objective* perspective. Unlike sports such as tennis and golf, where a flaw in technique can dramatically manifest itself in the form of a graceful lob over the back fence, or a beautiful hooked drive into the woods, faulty skiing technique is harder to detect, since you can commit a number of technical errors and still make it down the mountain, albeit with less speed, comfort, and style. To combat this, many have found it helpful to submit themselves to the periodic scrutiny of an independent and objective "mirror" in the form of a competent ski instructor. Yes, instruction is not the sole province of the beginner. You will find these brush-up sessions even more helpful if you use the same instructor (provided, of course, that he is competent and helping your skiing), since that person will be familiar with your deficiencies and will have worked with you enough so that you both can freely communicate, making reference to teaching aids and analogies that in the past have helped you through the rough spots in your technique. Another good vehicle through which to analyze your technique is the videotape machine, once a novelty but now standard equipment at many of the modern ski resorts. As we will discuss in the next chapter, the first step in curing your technical problems is to be aware of them—a goal more easily achieved through firsthand observation.

For me, skiing is . . .

Solitude,

Cutting up the powder,

Busting through the bumps, or . . .

ıst hotdogging it on a sunny afternoon,

Skiing is also: Pretty girls,

Winter carnivals,

Wine and cheese on the mountainside with your friends, and

A chance to play in a breathtaking environment.

A rare moment: the author after a fall!

Skiing can bring one to beautiful and unusual places, such as the rim of New Zealand's Ngurahoe Volcano (photo by Mike Halstead).

Actors in the never-ending drama of World Cup Competition: Swedish Champion Ingemar Stenmark,

Not everyone is fortunate enough to ski regularly with the champions—but there are reasonable substitutes.

Chapter Four

THE SECOND ELEMENT: AWARENESS

As we have observed, the obvious first and crucial step in solving any problem is making a determination that that problem in fact exists, and while this is particularly true in skiing, the task is made somewhat more difficult, since there are few external factors such as the speed, distance, and trajectory of a ball by which to measure your proficiency. It becomes important, therefore, that we find a competent and objective observer such as a videotape or ski instructor, or both, to point out exactly what we are doing improperly. The next, and sometimes most difficult, step is to accept these observations. I say difficult because what you may feel you are doing may differ radically from what you are doing in fact. An example of this phenomenon, which I have frequently observed, relates to the position of the arms during turns. As we shall discuss in considerably more detail, it is vital to the success of a clean carved turn that you keep your body weight over your skis throughout the turn. This is largely a function of strength and body position, with an emphasis on the latter. Where go the arms, so goes the upper body, and one of the most common bad habits, even among the very best of skiers, is to let the arms (particularly the arm on the inside of the turn) get behind the skier during the turn, with the result that the body weight is no longer properly distributed over the skis; this in turn results in a loss of control and a lack of preparation for the next turn. It would seem that the logical solution would be to merely hold the arms in front of your body as you make the turn. But, unfortunately, it's not that simple: The forward motion of your body over the snow and past the site of your original pole plant dictates that regardless of where your arm was when you planted the pole in the snow, you must drive that inside hand forward throughout the turn in order to maintain it in its proper position. Thus, in this instance, it takes a dynamic motion to maintain what outwardly appears to be a static position. In short, the forward thrusting of the inside hand as you complete the turn compensates for the "skiing by" effect by keeping your upper body faced more or less downhill—in a posture from which you will be well positioned to properly initiate the next turn—and the next, and the next, and the next . . .

Many skiers, particularly the self-taught and those who learned to ski during different eras, have skiing styles that, although they feel good, are riddled with bad habits that ultimately block their way to becoming expert skiers and enable them to ski competently only when things are going their way and conditions are ideal.

How do we rid ourselves of these deeply ingrained bad habits? Easy: In a manner of speaking, your mind is like a tape recorder to the extent that when you give it new input, you record over and simultaneously erase the older erroneous material. They say that you can't teach an old dog new tricks, but I disagree. The only difference between an old dog and a young dog is that the old dog's habits have become more deeply ingrained through repetition—but not beyond repair. But verbal instructions and/or visual images alone are not enough to change these bad habits. It is essential that you actually experience the feeling of doing it properly and repeat that experience with enough frequency so that you can bring back that successful feeling at will, not by intellectualizing its component parts, but, as said earlier, through the *Gestalt* or the total feeling of what it is like to do it right.

I have found, as I am sure many of you have, that our bad habits seem to surface at absolutely the worst time—for example, under the stress of competition. It has been my personal experience that the best way to perform well in a stressful situation is to concentrate on the primary goal—the matter at hand—for example, getting down the mountain as fast as possible, rather than the procedures involved—and leave the habit-changing and computer programming for less stressful situations. Many who have followed the successes I have been fortunate enough to have in skiing competition assume that I know no speed but full speed, not only in my racing but in my training and recreational skiing as well. This is simply not the case, and if you have observed me in my free skiing, particularly before and/or between the runs of a competition, you probably have noticed that I behave quite to the contrary —that I seem to ski in slow motion. The reason for this is simple: By making my turns slowly and deliberately, I can, absent the stress of competition or adverse skiing conditions, repeatedly experience the feeling of executing a near-perfect carved turn. The more often I experience this feeling, the more likely it is to become habit and therefore occur without conscious effort when I am skiing hard. The two things that should be remembered here are: First, your previous input, however erroneous, can be modified, and second, the more frequently your new program is replayed, the more enduring it will become and the more often it will surface during your spontaneous behavior.

Another discovery I have made, and one that is backed up by studies of psychologists and doctors of sports medicine, relates to the power of imagination or mental picturing as a learning device. The crux of this concept as applied to our sport is simple: You do not have to be on the snow to practice good skiing. Once you have actually felt what it is like to make a proper turn, you can replay that experience in your mind, recalling such vivid detail that you feel as though you are actually experiencing it. Of course, the success of this type of armchair practice is only good to the extent of your power of imagination and your commitment to recall vividly even the most minute details of your skiing experience. During the year in which I competed on the North American professional tour, I met a young American racer who, although he started skiing much later in life than a vast majority of his peers and, due to financial limitations, was unable to play the necessary game of "catch-up" during the summer months, did, nevertheless, show considerable improvement from one season to the next, even though he had not been on snow during the interim. When I asked how it was possible for him to accomplish this, he told me that, during the summer months, he drove a dump truck in order to raise money to be able to ski on the tour during the winters, and that each day, as he sat behind the controls, turning the steering wheel and alternately pumping the clutch, brake, and gas pedals, he played and replayed his mental picture of how it felt when he was making the best turns of his life at the end of the previous season.

As you recall, this chapter started out as a dissertation on the role that awareness plays in good skiing. Thus far we have focused on the importance of being aware of existing problems with your skiing technique and the means by which they can be remedied—namely, a mental picture of how those particular maneuvers are done correctly and a relaxed physical and/or imaginary repetition of those moves in order to imprint them upon your subconscious. Fortunately, and to its credit, skiing is not practiced in a vacuum where all things are constant, but in a dynamic environment where there exist a number of things that you should take into consideration so that your decisions and movements are based on all relevant input, not just isolated factors. Among other things, you should be aware of the following:

Your Body: Extending a bit from what was said earlier, I cannot emphasize enough the value of knowing what is going on with your body at any specific point in time. Although this information can be relayed to you from time to time by an objective source, you will usually have to rely on your senses and perceptions. Without this feel, it is difficult, if not impossible, to properly co-ordinate your body movements. Physical fitness contributes greatly to this body awareness, particularly the type of fitness derived through the stretching and relaxing yoga exercises described earlier.

Your Environment: It is also quite important for you to be aware of or "tuned into" the particular environmental circumstances under which you are operating. Is the snow hard or soft? Is its surface bumpy or smooth? Is the trail wide or narrow, winding or straight? How many other skiers are around? These are all important questions, the answers to which must be fed to your computer and stored for the appropriate moment. And, of course, awareness of the aesthetic aspects of the environment is, at least for me, a very important part of the skiing experience.

Your Equipment: Since your equipment forms the link between your body and the snow, it forms a vital component of your awareness package as well. Are your boots tight, your bindings holding firmly? Are your skis carving precisely and running smoothly?

I would like to stress that this "awareness inventory" is not something you should do at the beginning of the day, but rather as an ongoing process that feeds a continuous flow of information to your human computer. In short, practice becoming more aware of your *present* circumstances and, as you ski, calculate your responses, not according to a preconceived set of circumstances or what those circumstances were one hour, ten minutes, or ten seconds, ago, but what is occurring *here* and *now*. A bump or transition may look radically different twenty yards away than it will when you are on top of it, and your preconceived notion of what action will be appropriate when you reach it may well be obsolete when you are there. Open your senses. See, hear, feel, come alive, be aware!

Chapter Five

THE THIRD ELEMENT: RELAXED CONCENTRATION

Thus far I have told you that you must program yourself with the proper input regarding skiing techniques; that you must prepare yourself through relaxed imaginary and/or actual practice of those techniques; and that you must absorb a mountain of input regarding your skiing environment and situation up to and including the moment of action. At this point I would not be surprised if you have become impatient or angry with me. Presumably you bought this book with the hope that it would simplify and clarify matters for you and help you improve your skiing without first having to wade through the morass of jargon and theory all too prevalent in the other "how to's" of our sport. "How," you ask, "can I possibly consider this myriad of information and yet have the presence of mind to make good turns (let alone turn at all) without running off into the woods, totally perplexed by this overwhelming mass of information?" The answer is simple: You don't. If you have followed the steps outlined above, your computer will be fully programmed for action and ready to do the job—that is, if you will let it. How is this achieved? Through a positive attitude and relaxed concentration.

In many cases, a positive mental approach will mean the difference between success and failure. Let me give you an example. You are fishing by a fast-moving stream far back in the forest, just off an old logging road when, to your horror, your car keys suddenly drop through a hole in one of your pockets into the stream. Fortunately, the keys have come to rest underwater, but within reach. A few inches farther and they will slide into the deep channel of the stream to be swept off forever by the rushing waters. As you reach for them, a veritable parade of horribles floods your mind: One false move, and I will be in big trouble—these are my only keys; it is getting late, my car is locked, and it's miles to help. As you are thinking this, you grab for the keys. For a fleeting moment, you get hold of them, only to drop them and have them slide inches closer toward the edge. Now you are really worried. It is getting toward the end of the day, you are cold and wet, and one false move will mean the difference between a restful fishing weekend and an extremely unpleasant ordeal. You desperately grasp for the keys, this time brushing them farther down the bank where they are swept away by the torrent. Time for an instant replay: You drop your keys in the water but, although you realize the unpleasant consequences if they are not retrieved, you put them out of your mind, take a deep breath, at the same time practicing exactly what you will have to do to retrieve the keys, picturing a positive result rather than the multitude of negative possibilities. Then, paying strict attention to the matter at hand, and envisioning only success, you reach forward and grasp the keys.

There are many similar analogies that can be drawn from our everyday experiences, and I have told this story to emphasize the virtues of a relaxed, positive, and concentrated approach to problem-solving, one that is conducive to success in virtually every endeavor, skiing included.

What is concentration? To me, concentration means a total focusing of one's attention on the matter at hand. People often ask how I was able to become such a great skiing champion. My answer is simple: For years on end, I made winning ski races the No. 1 priority of my life, evaluating everything I did on and off the slopes in terms of whether or not it would help me achieve that end. This involved a constant sorting out of negatives and irrelevancies and a focusing of my attention on that which would result in the realization of that goal. This brings to mind the importance of timing as far as the focusing of one's attention is concerned. The correct time to concentrate on preparing your skis is when you are preparing your skis, not when you are trying to make good turns on the ski hill. Therefore you must not only concentrate, you also must concentrate on the here and now—specifically, that which you are trying to achieve at the given moment rather than what has occurred previously or what might happen in the future.

I am sure that most of you, at some point in your lives, have had an experience where everything seems to go your way—where it is almost impossible for you to do anything wrong. In skiing, this would be that beautiful day when, due to the sunshine, the company, the adrenaline rushing through your system, or a combination of these or other factors, you become "stoked," skiing "out of your head" with little thought to the niceties of technique, performing feats previously considered beyond your capabilities. What has happened is that the excitement or challenge of the moment has captured your attention, freeing your mind from conscious thought of the complexity of the task you are performing. You were no longer *trying* to ski correctly, you *were* skiing correctly. The power of the moment had taken your mind away from the conscious effort to ski properly and had allowed your subconscious to form a synthesis of all your previous experience and programming and translate it into correct responses to the circumstances.

How can this state be achieved without waiting for those rare occurrences? The answer: By relaxing, by maintaining a positive self-image (role-playing, if it helps), and by concentrating on the here and now—the matter at hand—not in a forced or anxious way, but in an attentive way. If you have ever "skied over your head" you have demonstrated to the world (and more importantly, to yourself) that performance of this caliber lies well within your range of capabilities. It then becomes obvious that it is only psychological factors that are holding you back. How then do we avoid "clutching" under pressure—using more muscle groups than are necessary to perform the task and making it more difficult than it is in reality? How can we consistently focus our attention on the present and allow our magnificently sophisticated organism with all its input and experience choose the appropriate muscle groups to do the job without our interference?

Over the years I have developed some devices that I find helpful to keep my mind uncluttered and in the present. Here are a few:

- As you are skiing, take the "awareness inventory" described in the previous chapter, paying particular attention to your body position, the terrain upon which you are skiing (and that which is immediately ahead of you), and the feel of your skis on the snow. Give special note to the position of your hands and arms. Are they forward, with the inside hand driving through on each turn?

- Rhythm and timing are most important to good skiing, particularly when you are making quicker, shorter-radius turns. I have found that rhythmic skiing is much easier when you are skiing to some type of cadence, real or imagined. In this connection, I have found it very helpful to hum or whistle a tune while I am skiing, varying the tempo simultaneously with that of my turns in response to changes in the terrain and/or my personal desires. Singing, humming, or whistling not only sets a cadence and establishes a rhythm for your skiing, it also quiets the mind and contributes to purposeful concentration. In addition, it reminds you to breathe.

- Audible and rhythmic deep breathing is vitally important to good skiing for more than one reason. First, deep breathing carries first to the lungs, and then to the extremities of the body, the oxygen necessary for peak performance. Ironically, the tensing up that often occurs when people are trying too hard involves not only the flexing and tightening of a number of facial muscles by and large unrelated to the performance of the act involved, but also a simultaneous holding of the breath at the precise moment when more, not less, oxygen is needed. I have found strong (to the point of being audible), deep breathing (in through the nose and out through the mouth, particularly in cold weather, when you must be careful not to burn your lungs) to be of vital importance, not only in supplying the necessary oxygen, but also as a device to keep the mind free of negative thoughts and focused on the present. The next time you ski, experiment a bit and you will find that your arm movements, your breathing (with or without musical accompaniment), and your turns can be co-ordinated into a rather single-minded "here and now" exercise in concentration that will bring pleasure and results to your skiing.

Relaxed concentration is an art that I feel you should take pains to develop, since it is an ability that can be applied not only to the benefit of your skiing, but to each and every one of your other endeavors as well. Take this chapter to heart and I am confident that you too will discover that life is not as difficult as we sometimes make it.

Chapter Six

THE FOURTH ELEMENT: PROPER ATTITUDE

One factor that can have a tremendous influence on the enjoyment and safety of your skiing is your basic attitude toward the sport. First, if skiing is to be preserved as a pleasurable hiatus from the cares of everyday life, you must keep it in the proper perspective—don't take it and yourself too seriously. To do so will cause you to try too hard which, as we know from our earlier discussions, is counterproductive and will transform what should be a fun activity into yet another trial of fire and water, with unhappiness and frustration as its just desserts. As you ski, make an effort to appreciate and enjoy *every* movement, good or bad. Even your worst blunders can be rationalized and appreciated, since they are part of the growing process. And by all means, take time to stop periodically and appreciate the natural beauty surrounding you, and experience the joy that emanates from the ambience and camaraderie of the very special social environment of skiing.

ATTITUDE AND SAFETY

As you know, many people are apprehensive about our sport, since they feel that it is inherently dangerous. As we discussed in the first chapter, there have been significant breakthroughs that have served to greatly reduce the likelihood of skiing injuries. One factor that we have not discussed, and one of vital significance in making skiing a safe and enjoyable sport, is the *human* factor. This brings us to our second major point regarding attitude: With a measure of common sense, accompanied by a respect for the rights of others, you can make skiing a safer and more enjoyable sport not only for yourself, but also for those around you. One of the most frustrating things for me in skiing is the absolute needlessness of most skiing accidents involving injury; needless because they could have been easily prevented through proper preparation by the skier of himself or his equipment or, in many instances, through a dose of good old common sense. If I were to write down every common-sense rule of skiing, this book would soon become an encyclopedia and a trusted bedside companion—not as interesting or informative reading, but as a sure-fire sleeping potion. I shall, therefore, concentrate on what I feel to be the three major principles that form the foundation of safe and enjoyable skiing: The Golden Rule of Skiing; Defensive Skiing; and a relative of the latter, Controlled Skiing. In this section, I will cite some examples from my own experience, some of which you may find humorous, some you may find sad, but most of which should prove enlightening.

KILLY'S GOLDEN RULE

SKI AROUND OTHERS AS YOU WOULD HAVE OTHERS SKI AROUND YOU

That, of course, will go down in history as Jean-Claude Killy's Golden Rule of Skiing. Unfortunately, in my attempt to be cute, I have unwittingly limited the scope of the rule. It should apply off as well as on the slopes. For example, many skiers fail to appreciate that skis and ski poles are sharp, pointed, and potentially dangerous objects as they cruise around the ski area, weaving back and forth through crowds of people with these potential implements of destruction casually slung over their shoulders. Perhaps I should retract Killy's Golden Rule and fall back on the original maxim: *Do unto others as you would have them do unto you.* Should we take a vote? Seriously, what is involved here is a basic respect for the rights and sensibilities of your fellow skiers, and if you test your actions in light of how you would react were they the acts of others (for example, cutting into the lift lines; skiing fast through a crowd of people; snapping the rope tow, T-bar, or Poma lift; bouncing the chair lift; shouting loudly; etc.), you will be a better person for it.

SKI DEFENSIVELY

As in the case of driving an automobile, a defensive attitude should be a guiding principle of the sport of skiing. By skiing defensively, I don't mean for you to ski timidly or not aggressively. As I have mentioned earlier, a positive and aggressive approach is an integral part of becoming a better skier, since it is through this aggressiveness that you push through old barriers and discover your full potential. Basically, defensive skiing involves an awareness of your surrounding environment, including other skiers, and an anticipation of changes in the environment and the actions of those other skiers. This naturally involves familiarizing yourself with the trails upon which you will be skiing and their condition. Most ski areas today have a relatively simple system to rate the difficulty of each run and provide relatively up-to-date reports on the snow conditions of those runs. I have known people who have blown a whole day of skiing by taking the expert lift by mistake and compounding that error by attempting to ski down a slope far too difficult for them at their particular stage of advancement. If this ever happens to you, see the lift attendant about a ride back down. It is better to risk embarrassment than injury and frustration. An obvious but often ignored rule of defensive skiing is that you should never ski so fast that you cannot stop within your field of vision; to ski fast into blind areas such as those caused by fog, transitions, large bumps, and so on is to court disaster.

SKI CONTROLLED

Controlled skiing is really part of defensive skiing, but is so important that I feel it should be mentioned separately. By controlled skiing I mean skiing within your capabilities, always maintaining the ability to change direction and/or stop when and where you want to. There is a great difference between skiing fast and skiing out of control, particularly when there are others present. I have said it before, and I'll say it again, because it's so important: In skiing, the name of the game is turning. Sure, heading your skis straight down the mountain and going hell bent for leather is a thrill, but you can't and won't want to do that all the time. Too few of us realize that turning is the chief means of controlling our speed—we can go faster or slower merely by changing direction. If you want to slow down or stop, you turn toward the hill or, as the instructors say, away from the fall line. In my opinion, many skiers hold back their progress by not viewing and utilizing turns as means by which to control the rate of their descent.

Confessions of an Unsafe Skier

- It is just plain stupid to try to ski fast through a crowd of people. You might get a ticket or, as was my case, that might be the least of your problems. The most unpleasant experience of my skiing career occurred when I was fifteen years old, blithely slaloming through a group of people—that is, until I struck a young girl, breaking her hip and putting her in the hospital for more time than I would like to remember. I don't mind telling you this story if it will help you learn from my experience rather than having to go through it yourself. I know that this incident cured me of at least one bad habit.

- When meeting another skier, remember that the downhill skier has the right-of-way. If you are at a junction of two runs, it is the person on the larger trail who has the right-of-way.

- Never ski fast near the trees. It doesn't take a mathematician to determine that if you are going forty miles per hour, ten feet from the trees, and you catch an edge at a thirty-degree angle, it won't be long before you are part of the scenery. The same applies to skiing near T-bars, Poma lifts, rope tows, etc., except that the consequences can be even worse, since you are endangering others as well as yourself.

- For obvious reasons, it is foolhardy to ski fast into a lift line or attempt to stop quickly above another skier. A junior racer (fortunately not me, in this instance) where I was once coaching attempted to stop above one of his companions, but did not quite make it—with the unhappy result that his friend was out for the season with two broken legs.

- If you have to show off, do it with a modicum of common sense. I will relate to you one of the most embarrassing experiences in my life, and one that did not happen all that long ago. In the late spring, when the snow is slushy and people are lying in the sun, the temptation to spray them with your rooster tail can be irresistible. But even the world's best skier can misjudge the situation and wind up looking like a buffoon. In this instance, trying to stop suddenly above some friends lunching at a sidewalk cafe, I caught an edge and wound up under the table eating someone else's hamburger!

- Ski lifts are not only convenient and excellent places to rest and/or socialize between runs, they are also potentially dangerous and no place for horseplay. Unfortunately, the best examples of how *not* to use the lifts come from my personal experience: Several years ago, at a World Cup race in Yugoslavia, when I found myself in a situation where there were ten minutes before my start and fifteen minutes left on the lift, it suddenly seemed like a smart idea to swing the chair and jump to a passing lift tower, skis and all. Unfortunately, this didn't work as well as I had planned. I dropped my poles and made a flying leap for the tower, grabbing onto one of the tower rungs like a flying Wallenda. As I jumped, my parka somehow got caught on the chair, violently wrenching me around the pylon. After what seemed like an eternity, my jacket finally ripped loose, leaving me hanging desperately by one hand, thirty feet above the rocks, my back to the pylon, and my leg so badly cut by one of the bolts on the pylon that I took stitches in three levels. Fortunately, the prerace adrenaline was pumping so vigorously that, ignoring statements of concern regarding my bloody leg, and unaware of the extent of my injury (I thought the blood was grease or paint from the pylon), I raced and won by two seconds. By the time I got to the bottom, the pain had caught up with me. Fortunately, this happened in the days of one-run giant slaloms. Needless to say, I was quite out of the running for the slalom of the following day, and it was at least two weeks before I could re-enter competition.

Do you think that I learned from this episode? No chance! Not long after this Yugoslavian adventure, while I was in Romania training for another World Cup race, the chair broke down on a very cold afternoon, leaving me stranded for some time about thirty feet above the snow. My brilliant solution to this dilemma was to hang my hands from the chair and drop. Once again I was foiled by my parka which, in this instance, had slid up over my face, completely blocking my vision. After a minute of hopeless (and embarrassed) struggle, I had to let go. To my great surprise and fortune, I landed in one piece—and not on the shoulders of a fellow skier.

One could draw two lessons from these experiences: Don't jump from chair lifts, or: Don't wear parkas on chair lifts. I would recommend the former as the more reasonable interpretation. If you are ever caught in a situation where the lift breaks down, be patient and wait. The area ski patrol is trained for such emergencies.

There are many varieties of ski lifts and many rules pertaining to their utilization that are well worth knowing, but a bit too tedious for me to attempt to chronicle at the present time. The point that should be remembered is that ski lifts are potentially dangerous pieces of machinery and can be very harmful if not respected as such. Along with the convenience of using the lifts comes the responsibility of knowing the rules governing their use and respecting those rules for your safety as well as that of your fellow skiers. If you have any questions regarding a particular lift, ask the lift attendant— that's what he's there for.

FATIGUE—A SUBTLE HAZARD

It is often said, with considerable validity, that the first and last runs are the most dangerous runs of the day; the first because (unless you have warmed up properly) your muscles are cold and stiff, and the last because you are tired. Cold, stiff muscles tear more easily than warm, loose ones and, when you are stiff, you lack the flexibility needed to respond quickly to and absorb terrain changes. When you are tired, you become careless, and your muscles lose some of their ability to resist shock and stress without injury to themselves and/or your bones. Although I do not have the statistics at my fingertips, I am willing to bet that a far greater percentage of accidents occur on the "one more run." A couple of years ago, I had an experience that graphically illustrates this point: It was the first race of the season—a time of reckoning and an opportunity to size up the competition. It is

The lift is a great place to rest and socialize between runs, but no place for horseplay.

also a time of reunion when racers from all over the world reconvene, and renew old friendships after a hiatus of up to four months. The site of this race was Vail, Colorado. Upon my arrival at the area, I walked up to the race hill to check out the conditions and see if I could spot any old acquaintances. I had been standing at the base of the mountain no longer than two minutes when I was spotted by a friend of mine, a young American racer: "Hi, Jean-Claude! Did you see my run? I worked hard all summer and, for the first time in my life, feel that I really have it together. My last run was the best one ever. It was going to be my last run of the day, but I'll take one more so you can see for yourself." Yes, my friends, before I could tell him that it is always good to end on a positive note and say that there would be plenty of time for me to see him ski during the race, he skated to the lift, rode up, and took that "one more." It was fast indeed—that is, until he caught a ski tip on a pole about three quarters of the way down, did a somersault, and landed on his shoulder, dislocating it and thereby putting himself out of the running for at least half the season. Need I say more? In addition to the fatigue factor, there is another reason for not taking that "one more" run: If you have skied the same run several times, you tend to become accustomed to it, paying increasingly less attention to the potentially dangerous variables as well as your own physical condition. This concomitant lessening of strength and vigilance can work to your detriment if you are not careful.

Fatigue can be a particularly formidable hazard on the first day of the season; on the first day of a vacation, if you are an occasional skier; and/or on short weekend trips, particularly after a rough week at the office and a long drive to the area. This is obviously aggravated if the drive is particularly long or if you have to adapt to new environmental conditions (for example, less oxygen, as is the case with so many of us who live at low altitudes and then ski in the mountains). So the next time you vacation in the mountains, I highly recommend that you spend the first day resting, getting organized and acclimated. This is the best time to do your shopping, write your postcards, organize your equipment, and buy your lift tickets. Save your skiing for the latter part of your vacation when you are well rested and more up to the task. On a related note, if you heed my preachings of Chapter One, you will find that stretching exercises and brief cardiovascular workouts are good ways to fight fatigue and accelerate the acclimatization process.

As is true with many things, too much skiing can be a bad thing. It is for this reason that I advise that you go for *quality,* not quantity. This will make your skiing more enjoyable and save your energy for the other pursuits so readily available at the ski resort. Don't push too hard. Try skiing hard for only a couple of hours at a time, punctuating your days with periodic breaks to enjoy your friends, the scenery, and the wonderful ambience of the mountains.

SKIING AND DRUGS

If you did not throw this book in the waste can during my earlier prescriptions for clean living or my daily exercise routine, you will probably do so now, since I am going to tell you that drinking and skiing are not always the best companions. Please bear with me—I realize I am being tough on you—but I feel it will be in your interest in the end. Let's face it: Wine, beer, brandy, or whatever are very much a part of the image and the ambience of skiing, and I certainly do not want to take any of the fun away. However, as in the case of driving, moderation should be the watchword, since, as your blood alcohol rises, your judgment decreases and your reaction time becomes slower, causing you to become more dangerous to yourself and to others. The second danger in skiing drunk is that you tend to overestimate your abilities and take chances that you would not ordinarily take while skiing with a "full deck."

Contrary to the myth so picturesquely embodied by the St. Bernard dog with a cask of brandy around its neck, it has been proven that alcohol does not keep you warm. On the contrary, it reduces your ability to resist the cold by robbing the body of valuable calories while it is being broken down. The warm feeling produced by a shot of alcohol is but a misleading illusion. Alcohol, my friends, is not the antifreeze it is cracked up to be; it is a depressant that shuts down your protective systems against the cold. Your body will fight the alcohol rather than the cold, and although you may feel good in the short run, you may well be hurting in the end. Skiing under the influence of drugs other than alcohol is an activity with which I have had no experience and is therefore a subject that I will not touch upon. I have had people tell me that it is an incomparable experience to "ski high." My reaction to this is simple: For me, skiing itself is a high, and anything that gets between me and that experience is a downer.

OTHER BITS OF SANITY AND INSANITY

- Night skiing is fun, but dangerous. Even with a full moon, you cannot see obstacles, particularly smaller ones, and distances can be particularly deceiving in the relative darkness. These dangers are often aggravated, since night skiing generally takes place in a party atmosphere when your judgment may not be up to par, you most likely are not adequately dressed, and your muscles are not up to the task. Temperatures also can be deceptive in this situation, and the possibility of getting lost greatly increased, with the chances of rescue greatly diminished since, if you get lost or hurt, it is likely there will be no one patrolling the slopes to rescue you.
- Stop only when it's safe; never on a cat track, in the middle of a crowded slope, under a bump, around a bend, or, for that matter, in any location where you cannot be seen from a reasonable distance.
- Don't tailgate. Race on the race course, not on crowded slopes. If two of you want to race, do it side by side, not by chasing each other down the hill.
- Don't cut into lift lines. If you see a ski school cut a line, don't feel badly; it is a perfectly acceptable skiing custom—and they have paid for the privilege.
- Respect race courses and/or training areas. Ski parallel to, not across the course—skiing across a course is a move that can be dangerous not only to you, but also to the racer, since he is concentrating on the course, not you.
- Try to appreciate the position of the other skier. For example, don't ski fast near a beginner, since he may become frightened and hurt himself, you, and others. By the same token, it is not cute to ski over the skis of another or make fun of the "turkeys." Remember, it was not all that long ago that you were in the same position, and there is always someone who is better than you.

- Don't block the trails when you are skiing with a group. Hold your discussions along the side, or at the bottom—beyond the runout, where you won't present a dangerous obstacle to others. For the same reason, don't block the loading and unloading areas of the lifts chatting with friends or putting on your skis.
- A Killy pet peeve: Although I love animals (my "best friend" is a sheep dog named Indian), I feel that it is dangerous and inconsiderate for us dog lovers to bring our pets to the slopes; dangerous and inconsiderate for other skiers—and the dog!
- Last but not least (and please forgive me for this cliché): Fill your sitzmark! That small crater you leave in the snow after a fall is analogous to leaving a large divot in the golf course, but different, and more serious, since others could be injured as a result of your thoughtlessness.

I would not blame you if, after hearing the various horror stories detailed in the preceding pages, you have evolved your own safety rule: Never ski near Jean-Claude Killy—he's a maniac! But believe me, I have experienced virtually every situation imaginable in the three decades I have been skiing, and let me tell you, I am a much better person and a safer skier because of it. I can only hope that you will live these experiences vicariously, learning from my mishaps rather than your own misfortune.

PART III

Situation Skiing

Chapter Seven

THE FOUNDATION

As I mentioned earlier, one aspect that separates skiing from most other sports and, to my way of thinking, makes it more interesting, is its element of diversity. Skiing is essentially a sport of *situations*—situations dictated by a variety of factors, such as terrain, weather, the presence of other skiers, the relative ability of those skiers, and so on. For me, this element of diversity, and the challenge of coping with and mastering the great variety of situations that one may encounter, are the primary reasons why skiing is my favorite sport.

Later in this book, I will focus upon twenty of these varied situations, many of which you frequently encounter if you are a regular skier, some of which you may not encounter in a lifetime. I have divided these situations into three logical categories: Situations of Climate, Situations of Terrain, and New Horizons—special situations you can seek out and experience to add depth to your skiing skill and more variety and enjoyment to your skiing experience. But first I will provide you with a cram course on the *foundation*—the advanced basics of the sport of which you should have a firm grasp before you tackle the variety and challenges of Situation Skiing.

Sprinkled throughout the following chapters you will find a series of captioned stop-action sequence photographs showing me performing the basics and tackling most of the twenty skiing situations. They say that a picture is worth a thousand words, and it is upon this premise, and in keeping with my belief that watching and imitating is every bit as effective (if not more effective) than reading as a learning device, that I have included these photos to underscore my points. I must caution you, however, that skiing is a *dynamic* activity involving fluid movement and constant adjustment to ever-changing circumstances. It is not a sport of poses, and it is for that reason that I am always reluctant to utilize still (as opposed to motion) photographs for instructional purposes. So keep this in mind as you examine the photographs that accompany the following chapters, and try to visualize not only what is occurring in the photos but also what has occurred *between* them.

BASIC BODY POSITION

Skiing is largely a matter of balance—a series of adjustments in varying degrees to changes in terrain. To be a good skier it is not necessary to have the balance of an acrobat, and I feel that anyone who can walk has enough natural sense of balance to become a decent skier. There are however, certain things that make it easier for one to stay in balance. The most important of these is knowing the correct way to stand on your skis. Rule No. 1: Use a wide stance for balance. To get a better feeling for what I am about to say, let's try the following experiment: Stand in the basic position that you would assume when skiing downhill (you can do this with or without your skis) and with your feet held together. Now ask a friend to push you to one side. If your feet remain together, he should be able to topple you with ease. Now try the same maneuver, but with your feet spread apart. The lesson is obvious: Your lateral stability increases proportionately to the distance between your feet.

Obviously, we cannot always ski with our feet three feet apart. Among other things, this would cause us to put far too much weight on the inside edges of our skis. The optimum position for lateral stability, therefore, is one in which the legs are more or less perpendicular to the ground, and the outside of the feet are about the same distance apart as the width of the hips. When you ski with your feet glued together, you are, in effect, trying to balance on the point of a triangle. By spreading your feet apart, you broaden this into a rectangular base, converting your basic stance from a tightrope walk to a relatively comfortable and stable position.

THE BASIC BODY POSITION: Relaxed but ready.

One of my major problems during my early years on the French team was that I was prone to frequent falling. My coach at the time, M. Honre Bonnet, recognized that I was falling due to a lack of balance, and the reason that I was losing my balance was that I was attempting to race with my feet together, a posture that limited my "balance base" and interfered with the natural independent working of the legs. Prior to that time it was considered not only stylish, but also technically correct, to ski with the feet glued together. Once I understood that for any style to have value, it must be functional as well, I began to analyze my technique, not in terms of aesthetic beauty, but as a utilitarian application of the laws of physics. After a considerable amount of experimentation, I found that the best stance for me was one with my feet six to eight inches apart, seldom any closer than that, but often wider, as in the case of skiing a very steep slope. For this reason, it is my suggestion that you learn to ski with your feet comfortably apart and learn to appreciate that utility, not style, should be the watchword of good skiing.

In the above photograph, you see my basic running position, the base from which I execute all of my skiing maneuvers. If I had to describe this position in three words I would use these: *RELAXED BUT READY*. But this I mean that the whole body must remain relaxed and supple so that it may act as a giant shock absorber to absorb irregularities in the terrain. Note how my ankles and knees are flexed, and my upper body (through the forward position of my hips) remains over my feet and relatively perpendicular to the surface of the snow. This position serves a dual purpose: It keeps me ready to absorb sudden changes in the terrain, and it keeps my weight over my feet despite my forward movement so that I may, at all times, maintain control over my skis—an element of control that would be lost should my weight get behind my boots. This natural, relaxed, and upright posture serves a third and very useful purpose: It allows me to ski much longer without getting tired than would be the case if I were to try to ski in a slumping-forward or a sitting-back position. Although it is difficult to tell from this photograph, my weight is right where it should be—right over the arches of my feet. Under ideal conditions, your weight should be poised as it would be if you were sliding down the hill on your ski boots alone—that is, with no significant forward or backward pressure on the tops of your ski boots. In other words, don't use your skis as crutches. Study this position carefully and practice it in front of your bedroom mirror before you hit the slopes. Notice again the forward position of my hips and the very slight forward angle of the upper body relative to the surface of the snow. The greatest single technical deficiency I see among skiers (up to and including top racers) is a dropping of the seat and a forward bending at the waist, both of which tend to lock the skier into an ungainly posture that is not only more tiring, but also a very difficult position from which to execute quick and economical maneuvers.

THE POLE PLANT

It is amazing how few skiers realize the importance of a proper pole plant in making turns. Every time I make a turn, I use my poles to good advantage. So should you. The pole plant is crucial for several reasons: First, it serves as a platform to help me unweight the skis so that I can shift them into position for the next turn. Second, the planted pole serves as a timing device, since I know that the instant my pole jabs the snow, it is time to start my skis turning in the new direction. Third, the planted pole serves as a pivot point around which the skis will describe an arc. Finally, as we will see in more detail later, the pole action, particularly the driving forward of the inside hand, keeps the body in the proper position to initiate the next turn.

In the photograph p. 112, I have just completed a left-hand turn and am in the process of planting my right-hand pole in the snow in anticipation of a similar turn to the right. This photograph was taken in a sequence of very quick short-swing turns, each well out of the fall line. Note the forward position of my arms and hence the forward or downhill-facing position of my upper body in relation to my skis which, at this phase of the turn, are nearly perpendicular to the fall line. Note also the significant amount of weight I am placing upon my pole in order to give me the sufficient unweighting to unlock the edge set of my left-hand turn and free my skis so that, through a right shift with my knees and a simultaneous forward thrust with my right-hand pole, I may bring them around and into position for the next turn.

It is also important to know *where* to plant the pole, a spot that varies with your speed and position relative to the fall line. In general, you should never plant your pole farther forward than about one foot behind the tips of your skis, or farther back than about opposite the middle of the feet (as is the case in the accompanying photograph, where I am making rather abrupt turns at a relatively low speed). Obviously, you must always plant the pole on the downhill side of your

THE POLE PLANT: The foundation from which good turns are started—and completed.

skis—on the side that will be the inside of your next turn—about one foot away from your skis when skiing close to the fall line, and more as you come closer to a position that is perpendicular with the fall line. As I mentioned earlier, and will continue to point out throughout the coming situations, you should (except in a traverse) try to keep your arms (and hence your upper body) pointed down the fall line. Since you are moving forward over the snow, it is easy (even though you had planted your pole well in front of you to initiate the turn) to ski by that planted inside pole, with the result that your arm is pulled back, twisting your upper body out of position. To avoid this, you must remember that when making a turn, you should keep your outside hand (my left arm in the photograph) forward in order to be properly prepared for when you will use that arm as the inside pivot point for the next turn, at the same time keeping your inside (or pivot arm) not only forward, but also *driving forward throughout the turn* to compensate for your forward movement over the snow. If you allow that inside arm to get behind you, it will cause you to sit back and lean into the hill, a position from which it is almost impossible to carve a turn and from which you will have to make a major adjustment in body position in order to be ready for the next turn. In order for your poles to work properly for you, they must be of the proper length; they should pass an inch or two under your armpit when you are standing upright on solid ground (poles standing on their tips, not buried to their baskets in the snow). If it will help, I stand five feet, eleven inches tall, and use a fifty-one-inch pole. Choose the length that is appropriate for you, but remember: If your poles are too long, they will have a tendency to throw you back; if they are too short, they will cause you to bend at the waist—both undesirable positions for the reasons we have discussed above. Think of the pole plant as a commitment to turn. You spot the place where you want to turn, you prepare, and when you reach this spot, you make your move—a decisive pole plant: Pow! You unweight, change your edge, and are off in a new direction almost before you know it!

UNWEIGHTING

Let me try to clear up some of the confusion about unweighting. First of all, unweighting is a movement on your part (or an interaction between you and the terrain) that results in reducing the amount of weight you are placing on your skis. The primary objective of unweighting is to allow you to shift the position of your knees laterally and thereby transfer your weight from one set of edges to the other and thus initiate the next turn. There are two kinds of unweighting: up-unweighting and down-unweighting. Very simply, up-unweighting is unweighting that results from the inertia caused by an upward movement of the body, while down-unweighting is the result of a sudden down movement of the body mass.

Let's experiment. Standing in an erect position, bend your knees and then suddenly spring up. If you jumped vigorously enough, your feet left the ground and you have just given a graphic demonstration of up-unweighting. Now stand erect with very little bending in the knees and suddenly bend the knees and drop the hips. The resultant lessening or total release of pressure between your feet and the ground was caused by down-unweighting. Back to the slopes. I would have to say that up-unweighting is the most common means used by most skiers, although as you become more proficient, your unweighting becomes more subtle and you tend to use the two interchangeably, depending on the circumstances. In the previous section, I pointed out that one of the functions of the pole plant is to initiate, yes, *up*-unweighting. In the photograph that accompanies that section, my knees are coiled, my pole is planted forcefully in the snow, and I am just beginning to initiate the up movement that will result in the unweighting of my skis and the movement of my knees forward and to the right to begin my right-hand turn. In most situations, a moderate but quick up motion (with the skis remaining on the snow) will produce enough unweighting to get a turn started. Actually, the amount of unweighting depends less on the amount of up movement than it does on the speed and forcefulness of execution, and what you should strive for here is a small but quick and explosive movement. Although down-unweighting tends to unweight the skis for a shorter period of time than up-unweighting, it generally will, if properly executed, loosen the grip and allow for a quick edge change. When I analyze films of myself on a slalom course, I see that I spring up when I have the time, and drop down when time is short. There are some times when you need hardly unweight at all, such as on hard snow when your skis can skid around easily, and in the bumps which, as we will explore later in detail, will do a good part of your un-weighting for you if your timing is right. On the other hand, the converse is true in soft snow, particularly deep powder, where an exaggerated amount of up-unweighting is required to shift from one turn to the next.

THE SYNTHESIS: THE PERFECT TURN

> *Whoever thinks a faultless piece to see,*
> *Thinks what ne'er was, nor is, nor e'er shall be.*
> POPE, "Essay on Criticism"

Mr. Pope was probably right. Perfection in skiing, like in any other discipline, is an absolute toward which we strive, an ideal that is probably unattainable, since our standards are ever-changing; that which may be considered perfect in the present frame of reference will most likely be considered quaint and elementary at a future point in time. What we must do, therefore, is strive to come as close as we can to that ever-changing absolute.

One of the reasons why I very much enjoyed the winter I spent racing on the North American pro tour was the spirit of buoyant camaraderie that existed among the various competitors. Since the pro tour involves a format of man-against-man dual giant slalom and slalom races, run on very hard or icy snow, one of the prime prerequisites for success is the ability to carve quick and efficient turns—in both directions. With the competition as intense as it was, and races being won and lost by thousandths of a second, it is not difficult to understand how the preoccupation of most came to be "working on that turn" to the point that one acquaintance, tongue in cheek, described the essense of his existence as nothing less than a "quest for the perfect turn." Let's face it: Turning is what skiing is all about, and the closer one can come to executing a "perfect" turn at will, the closer he will be to becoming the "perfect" skier.

For the purpose of our discussion, however, a perfect turn will mean a relaxed, almost effortless turn in which the skis do not slide sideways in relation to the vector of the turn, but rather trace two clean parallel arcs, as if the skier were locked in a set of tracks. Perhaps a better analogy would be to the precisely carved turns of a championship figure skater. Under the traditional instructional approach, we would describe for you, in rather esoteric terms, the various movements you must pull together in order to make such a turn. I am, however, going to try something different, which I hope will be more helpful in programming you with the necessary information to be able to execute the various maneuvers we shall discuss. I will give you a description from my point of view—a "Killy-eye view," if you will—of the process I go through while making a carved turn and what it feels like to execute such a maneuver. Then, to complete the picture, we will show you what the properly executed maneuver looks like from the perspective of an objective observer by providing stop-action sequence photographs with an appropriate description of the action.

Now that I have defined my terms and outlined my methodology, we will discuss the difference between a modern carved turn and the time-honored parallel christie. The main difference between these two turns is that in the former (at least in its properly executed form), the skier changes direction by carving an arc with his skis rather than alternately grabbing and releasing his edges and thereby skidding them around the turn.

Before getting too deeply into the dynamics of the perfect turn, it might be helpful to digress a bit and briefly outline for you the evolution in skiing technique that has led up to the modern carved turn. In this connection, it is interesting to note the variety of means that people have employed over the ages to turn their skis. In fact, I have witnessed three distinct phases in the evolution of skiing technique during my lifetime alone: the rotation method, the counterrotation (or reverse-shoulder) method, and the modern carved turn.

Rotation

If I were to make a right-hand turn under the antiquated rotation method, I would actually wind up for that turn by cranking my body to the left and would then swing (or rotate) my upper body in the direction in which I wanted to turn (in this case, the right), leading my left or outside hand, and hoping that the rest of my body and, most importantly, my skis would follow. The rotation method (which, to many be-

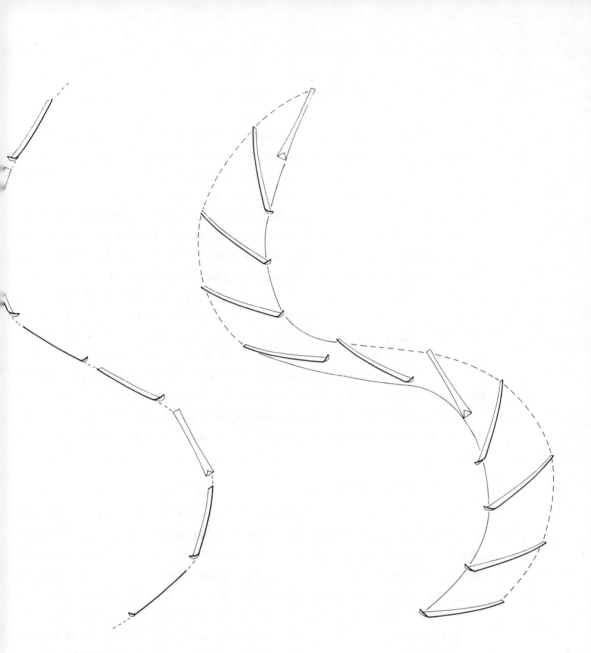

CARVED   SKIDDED

The difference between ski tracks produced by a carved turn and a skidded turn.

ginners, seems to be the most obvious way to turn the skis) is the most tiring and least effective and efficient way of turning, since it requires not only an anticipatory windup, but also a follow-through that twists the skier out of position for the next turn.

Counterrotation

The counterrotation or reverse-shoulder technique grew out of an application of the basic law of physics that for every action there is an equal and opposite reaction. Picture yourself sitting on a revolving stool, such as you would find in a bar, with your feet pointed forward and your arms out in front as if you were skiing. Suddenly swing your arms to the right. Which way do your legs go? To the left. In effect, your body behaves as though it had a swivel at the waist. Remember the Twist? Applied to the ski slopes, this phenomenon produces what we refer to as "turning power" and forms the basis for the counterrotation technique, in which an unweighting of the skis followed by a twist of the upper body in one direction produces a turning of the lower body and the skis in the opposite direction. Although this technique became more subtle and sophisticated over the years (largely through a fairly steady evolution toward less movement of the upper body out of the fall line—hence the expression "maintain a quiet upper body"), it did, for many years, remain the most efficient way to make our skis change direction.

The Modern Way

It was during this period of evoluton, and due primarily to the development of more flexible skis with more pronounced bottom and side cambers, that leading skiing technicians first began to achieve the sensation of carving rather than sliding their skis. However, it was not until the coming in the middle sixties of more flexible and resilient Fiberglas skis that carved turns came to become the rule rather than the exception—at least in the technique of racers and leading ski teachers. As we indicated in our section on equipment, certain properties of the newer Fiberglas skis allow the ski itself to do a lot of the turning for the skier, primarily by allowing the skier to make a more efficient utilization of the laws of physics.

The first and foremost difference between today's carved-turn technique and the counterrotation method is that with the latter method the skier remains more squared to his skis: In making a right turn, the inside or right ski would remain ahead of the outside or left ski but, in this instance, by only a couple of inches. In this technique, the inside knee, hip, and shoulder should also be forward the same amount as the inside ski. This is what we call being squared to your skis. The second difference is that in the modern carved turn there is more of an emphasis upon a forward pressing of the knees, ankles, and hips and little or no emphasis upon a twisting or counterrotation of the upper body. It remains necessary, of course, to angulate—to have the knees bent in the direction of the turn so that the proper set of edges is biting into the snow—but this angulation is more subtle and is coupled with more of a forward motion of the knees than was the case in the earlier technique.

It would be logical to ask at this point how, if you do not twist your body, are you able to bring the skis around. The answer is simple, but is not apparent unless you understand the workings of modern ski equipment. I will try to put this as simply as possible: The increased side camber and flexibility (a characteristic that is becoming more pronounced with each passing year) of the new Fiberglas skis makes it possible (depending upon such factors as the body position and speed of the skier, the angle of his skis, and the amount of pressure he places upon them) for the skier, relying on his forward movement and the resistance of his edges against the snow, to bend the skis in a arc that will correspond to the curvature of his turn. The harder the pressure, the tighter the arc, the sharper the turn.

Beginning to get the message? Therefore, what we used to achieve through a twisting of the body, we now achieve by riding fairly squarely over the skis, having the knees at the proper angle, and applying the right amount of forward pressure throughout the turn. Before ending this discussion, I would like to point out that the modern ski is not only more flexible, but also more resilient, and (particularly in the harder and quicker turns) the rebounding of the ski will alone provide most, if not all, of the unweighting necessary to enable the skier to shift into position for the next turn. To sum it up: Less sideways twist plus more forward drive equal less skidding and more carving. Now that I have you totally confused, let's take a "Killy-eye view" of that "perfect turn" we have heard so much about.

1

2

3

THE PERFECT TURN — A KILLY-EYE VIEW

The day is sunny, the mountain freshly groomed. I am traveling at about twenty-five miles per hour and have just come off a steeper part of the mountain onto a relatively flat area which, with the exception of some tracks and an occasional row of loose snow left by the packing machine, is as smooth as a billiard table. My objective: the perfect turn! In photo 1, I am in the final stage of a left turn when I hit the transition from the steep to the relatively flatter surface. In order to prevent myself from being thrown forward by the transition and, at the same time, to position myself for the extra unweighting that will be necessary to initiate my next turn during the compression of the transition, I sit back slightly, drop my seat, and bring the tip of my right pole forward in anticipation of the pole plant that I will use as a base from which to initiate the coming turn. Now that I have successfully absorbed the transition and made my pole plant (photo 2), I shift my knees slightly to the right and bring my right knee, hip, and shoulder subtly forward and come up and forward with my hips to a position from which I can exert steady pressure on my knees and ankles—pressure that I can monitor to keep my skis carving throughout the turn. Once I have initiated the turn (photo 3), my task is relatively simple: to hold a relaxed and upright body position similar to the basic body position that we described earlier, but with the exception that I am leading slightly with my inside ski knee, hip, and shoulder (photo 4). As I turn, I maintain a mild inward angulation of my knees and, since I am turning against a slight bank, a slight banking or leaning of my body into the turn. My task now becomes very similar to that of steering a race car around a banked racetrack (photo 5). To keep my body square over my skis, and to keep them carving throughout the turn, I keep my left hand forward and drive my right hand forward as I progress around the arc, applying just enough forward pressure with my knees to keep my weight over my feet throughout the turn and transmit the right amount of torque to the skis to cause them to bend to the desired arc of my turn and keep from side-slipping. As I begin to round the curve, leaving the fall line and heading toward a traverse (photo 6), I begin to feel the increased efforts of gravity and centrifugal force, which I offset through angulation and increased resistance through an application of forward pressure on the knees and ankles (photo 7). It is this basic body position, with my knees pressed forward and my hips over my boots, which allows me to accurately monitor my forward pressure to the extent necessary to keep the skis carving in the desired arc (photo 8). In the last photo of this series, I have completed a full turn and am traversing to my right with my knees bent slightly forward and into the slope and my left arm coming forward ready to initiate the pole plant that will serve as the platform and centerpoint of my next, well-*near*-perfect turn.

5

6

7

8

9

Putting It All Together: Linked, Carved Turns

At this point you should have a fairly clear idea as to how to go about making a good carved turn. However, one turn does not an expert make, and you must be able to put several together at will before you will begin to be considered a master. The expression "he (or she) can turn both ways" seems at first to be a jocular understatement, but think about it—there are really not that many people who can turn with equal skill in both directions. I would guess that this is due to a number of reasons: First, unless we are perfectly ambidextrous, one side of our body dominates the other. Thus in running, and in skiing, a right-handed person tends to lead with the right arm and left leg. The effect of this on skiing is that right-handed skiers tend to have a much easier time turning to the right than they do in the opposite direction. The converse is obviously true in the case of the left-handed. Many sports, such as tennis, golf, and bowling, place a heavy emphasis on the dominant side of the body. This tends to make the skiing problem even more pronounced, since these one-sided sports will build up certain muscle groups at the expense of others and thus exacerbate the difference. That is one reason why I prefer ambidextrous sports such as water skiing, soccer, cycling, handball, and running as conditioners for skiing. However, as I said before, I do not want to discourage you from participating as much as possible in your favorite sport, even though that sport may not have a direct application to skiing, since it will surely contribute to your basic level of physical fitness, and the enjoyment factor will spur you on to greater heights. How then do you compensate for this one-sidedness? We know that the first step in curing any problem is to become aware of it. We also know that the best way to do this is to examine exactly what the various parts of your body are doing through a sense of body awareness and/or the eyes of a competent objective observer. The next step is to program your computer with images of what you must do, practice that maneuver in reality and/or in your mind until it is firmly recorded, and then do it.

Shortswing is nothing more than a series of shorter-radius versions of the carved parallel turn, which we have discussed in considerable detail earlier in this chapter. Although these turns are obviously easier to execute on a smooth and relatively flat slope, they can be done on virtually any type of terrain, provided you make the proper adjustments—adjustments we will discuss in more depth later in this book. The basic elements of shortswing are as follows:

- *Basic Body Position*—Relaxed with arms forward, hips forward, knees and ankles slightly bent, and skis slightly apart for balance. One difference between these quicker, linked turns and the wide, arcing turn we discussed earlier is that, since you do not complete each turn into a traverse, your upper body should remain quiet and face pretty much downhill through every phase of the turn.

- *Decisive, Rhythmic Pole Action*—The pole plant becomes the primary means of unweighting in these rapid-fire, tighter-radius turns. The driving through of the inside hand after the pole has been planted serves to keep your weight over your skis and the skis carving throughout the turn. It also is the means by which you keep your arms in a forward position, ready for what's to come. Again, it is important, particularly in this type of skiing, to set a cadence or rhythm to time the initiation of each turn and keep the mind from being distracted by negative thoughts and/or overattention to detail.

- *Knee and Ankle Action*—Just following my pole plant, and concurrent with the forward driving of my inside hand, I press forward with my knees, putting just enough pressure on my skis to make them carve the desired turn. As I carve the turn, approximately 65 per cent of my weight is on the outside ski and 35 per cent is on the inside ski.

1

2

3

4

5

6

SHORT SWING

I have just skied onto a relatively flat and well-groomed slope, which looks like an ideal place to make a tight series of linked, short-swing turns. In photo 1, I am in the final stage of a sharp right-hand turn, which I have used to control my speed and set up for the series of turns to follow. Note my body position: hands forward; upper body facing downhill; weight over my skis; knees angulated into the hill and pressed forward to complete the right-hand turn, at the same time coiled for the up-unweighting that will initiate my left-hand turn; my left hand forward and reaching for the pole plant that will initiate that turn. A split second later (photo 2), I have planted the pole and am using it and the up motion of my knees to free my skis so that I may shift them into position for the next turn. Again, in this photo, and in each of the following photos, note that my upper body remains quiet and facing down the hill while most of the work in turning is done through the forward and inward motion of my knees. This point is particularly well illustrated by a comparison of photos 2 and 7. In photo 3, my skis are nearly totally unweighted, and I use this brief op-portunity to move my knees to the left and in position for the next turn. Once my skis are fully weighted (photo 4), I complete the turn by driving through with my knees and hips (photo 5), taking care not to allow my inside hand to trail behind. With the turn nearly completed (photo 6), I bring the tip of my right pole forward for the pole plant (photo 7) (note that my arm was already in position), and, of course, my next turn (photo 8). At this point I have begun to establish a rhythm, inhaling as I unweight, exhaling as I drive forward through each turn. It now becomes quite automatic: my hands punching forward, followed by a thrusting of my knees and hips, first in one direction, and then in the other; my upper body quiet and facing down the hill; my sense of balance undisturbed, since the shocks from my turns and the terrain beneath my feet are being absorbed by my knees and ankles, not my upper body. My eyes are focused about two turns ahead, planning the route I will take down the mountain, feeding visual information to my computer so that my body will react correctly when I reach that point.

7

8

When All Else Fails: The Emergency Stop

As I said earlier, turning is what skiing is all about. Turning is not only a fun exercise and a means of determining the route you will take down the mountain or through the gates; it is also a means of controlling your speed. Once you realize this, and once you are able to make a solid turn (however basic) in either direction, most of the fears you may associate with skiing should fall by the wayside. However, once in a while, even in the case of the most experienced skiers, some unexpected obstacle, the intervention of another skier, the catching of an edge, or some other unforeseen occurrence may cause you to lose control, gaining enough momentum so that it is impossible to resume your earlier pace. What then? Well, the first thing you should do, provided it can be accomplished safely, is to end this helter-skelter journey down the fall line by making a wide turn into a traverse—preferably away from the center of the hill. If you wish to come to a complete stop in order to gather your wits, complete that turn into an uphill traverse, and you will eventually stop. What if you do not have enough time to make this graceful retreat from disaster? When all else fails, I recommend the emergency stop.

THE EMERGENCY STOP

The emergency stop (or hockey stop, as it is often called) is very similar to the parallel stop that a hockey player makes when he must quickly change direction. To make an emergency stop, you simply make a sharp turn in whichever is the best direction under the circumstances and, instead of completing that turn by driving forward with the knees and hips, you get into a position where your skis are skidding sideways nearly perpendicular to the fall line (essentially a rapid side-slip—see photo 1), with your upper body facing fairly well downhill, and when you are ready, you bite as hard as you can into the hill with your edges through a great deal of angulation and forward bending of the knees (photo 2, 3) and grind

1

2

3

4

to a screeching halt! (photo 4). Since you are traveling with considerable momentum, it is possible that if you don't make the proper compensation, your feet could stop while your upper body "keeps on truckin'" with what can best be described as a less than pleasant outcome. To avoid this, I begin the stop by leaning into the hill, extending my body almost straight, with my downhill or outside hand raised high (photo 1), and then use my body as a shock absorber (photos 2–3) to soak up the energy of the stop. Take care not to lean too far into the hill while executing this maneuver or your skis will slip out from under you, and you will be in simi-

lar trouble. If you are moving slowly, this move can stop you almost on a dime; but if you are moving fast, you will experience some sideways skidding before you can break your momentum and come to a full stop. The emergency stop is a maneuver that is best practiced on an easy slope when you are not under pressure. Although you will probably use it only when you have to—and I hope that will not be too often—it is definitely a good move to have in your bag of tricks.

THE FOUNDATION   127

Falling—It's Not as Bad as It Looks

Before we venture further, I would like to make a few comments on that nemesis of every skier, particularly those who have just begun or who are about to take up the sport: falling. One of the reasons that many people who would really enjoy skiing do not take it up is that they fear the pain and injury that they feel are the inevitable results of taking a spill on skis. For the same reason, many long-time skiers inhibit their development because they are unwilling to take the risks necessary to expand their skiing horizons. Friends, you must believe me: Falling is not as bad as it looks. Your forward motion over the snow, the inclined surface of the slope, the relatively soft snow surface, and modern safety bindings guarding your limbs all combine to make falling an innocuous part of skiing. Every skier falls; even I do.

When falling, even in a high-speed "egg beater," the main thing to remember is to not fight it; relax, stay loose, and be confident that you are going to come out okay, because that is what will happen ninety-nine times out of one hundred. If you are going slowly, and feel that you are about to fall, start by sitting back as if you were going to sit down. Obviously, you do not want to sit on the tails of your skis, or you would soon become a human toboggan. Keep your hands up and your poles pointed behind you so that the poles will not catch and be jammed into you. Now move your seat off to the side and sit down on the snow. With most of your weight now on your posterior, you can keep your skis parallel, their tips free from the snow to avoid catching and digging in. If you are traversing, sit down on the uphill side of your skis and you won't have as far to fall. If you fall at higher speed, try to keep your skis behind you and up in the air so that they do not catch and twist your legs. Once you have regained your equilibrium, the friction of your ski clothing against the snow and the dragging of your arms should soon slow you down. In this connection, I highly recommend that you wear the newer "antigliss" ski clothing which, unlike the old "wet look" nylon, is designed to bring you to a quick and safe stop. And, yes, please forgive me for not providing you with a series of photos on this subject.

Switzerland's Women's Champion, Lise-Marie Morerod, and

American Slalom and Giant Slalom Ace Phil Mahre—or is it twin brother Steve?

In the electrifying spectacle of pro racing, it is not hard to see who is ahead . . .

And why!

1976 and 1977 World Pro Champion
Henri Duvillard.

Name the mystery champion.

The wild and woolly world of freestyle:
The moguls,

Ballet,

And aerials:
Yes, that's a lady freestyler, Lea Hillgren,
executing a "back moebius flip".

Other "New Horizons":
Cross country and touring,

Ski mountaineering,

Glacier skiing,

And hang gliding: Wow, but watch out!

They say that a picture is worth a thousand words. So, why spoil this one with a caption? (photo by Jean-Claude Killy).

A Note on Injury

If by chance you are injured, try not to get excited—what is done is done! By getting emotional, you burn up energy that you will need to fight the pain and the cold. Almost all of the modern skiing areas have well-organized and trained ski patrols who will not leave you alone for long. While you are waiting for the patrol, try to stay relaxed and keep as warm as possible. Don't hesitate to borrow someone's jacket to provide that needed extra warmth. You are not being a baby; you are being smart. By the same token, if you find someone injured on the slopes, cover him to keep him warm and send someone to notify the ski patrol. It is then a good idea to stay with that person, keeping him calm and making sure he is in the most comfortable position. Beware, however, that you should *never* move an injured person any more than is absolutely necessary. If his spine is injured, you could very easily cause irreparable harm to his nervous system, including paralysis and even death.

Finally, don't be embarrassed to be taken down the mountain in a toboggan if there is any chance that your injury is serious. That is what the ski patrol is for. To underscore this point, let me tell you what happened to one of my good friends, an expert skier and a ski and winter sports promoter of some renown who once upon a time fell and twisted his ankle while skiing near the site of a skiing competition. Rather than risk the embarrassment of being needled by his friends and associates as he rode to the bottom in the ski patrol toboggan, he chose to ride piggy-back courtesy of a well-meaning but not too bright friend of his. As it went, the friend, unaccustomed to the extra weight, lost control of his skis and ultimately hit a large bump at a relatively fast clip, launching both of them into space. The result: Instead of a sprained ankle, my friend wound up in the hospital with a compound fracture, and his benefactor with a dislocated hip. Need I say more?

At this point I have presented you with enough information to become a good skier. Now I want to tell you what you have to do to become an *expert* skier, one who can handle himself competently in all types of conditions and situations. If you have absorbed everything I have said so far, you are well on your way, and all you really need to do is be bold, venture out, and experience the wide variety of possibilities that are open to you in our favorite sport. The purpose of the remaining pages will be to make you aware of the great number of options available and to show you the little nuances you can employ to cope with and get the most from them. As you read and digest the following materials, keep in mind that although we will focus upon what should be done differently in these various situations, the basic fundamentals provided earlier will nevertheless apply—unless, of course, we state otherwise. It has taken me a lifetime of skiing experience to learn these little tricks, and I hope that by relaying them to you in this format, I can shorten your journey to expert skiing.

Chapter Eight

SITUATIONS OF CLIMATE

Although variety is the spice of life, and many of the pleasures of skiing spring from its great variety of environment, one must nevertheless be aware of and know how to cope with the various situations he can encounter while practicing the sport. In short, what makes skiing interesting, can also make it frightening and dangerous unless you know what you are doing. In alpine skiing, particularly in the mountains, the climate can either enhance the conditions under which one skis or make them extremely trying, and one extreme can change to the other sometimes in an hour or less. Thus what may start out to be a sunny afternoon with hard-packed slopes can, in a very short time, change into a blinding blizzard with subzero temperatures and enough powder to stall a snow cat. When the conditions are less than optimal—which is most of the time—you are faced with two options: to learn to cope, or to become a fair-weather skier. I feel quite sorry for those who opt for the latter, since they really don't know what they are missing by their refusal to accept the challenge of skiing's ever-changing environment. If you do decide to accept this challenge, let awareness be your watchword.

A classic example of a person who exhibited a lack of environmental awareness is the young racer friend of mine who tried to lick the frost off his metal ski pole at twenty-five below zero—a move almost as foolish as that of another friend of mine who, while on a bird-hunting expedition, chose to relieve himself on an electric fence! Be aware, accept the challenge. By learning to cope with and enjoy the bad days, the good days will seem all that much better—better by comparison and better because of the new abilities you will develop on the training ground of adversity.

Situation 1: Powder

If you have done it, you know. If you haven't, you must take my word for it: Deep-powder skiing can be one of life's most exciting experiences. For me, only skiing very fast can compare with the thrill and exhilaration of cutting a new track through freshly fallen powder snow. Unfortunately, too many skiers shy away from powder, thinking it is beyond their ability. This is perhaps due to unpleasant experiences they had as beginners. Also, on hard snow, you may make a mistake and get away with it. If you catch an edge, for instance, it is nothing to quickly pull your ski back in line. In powder, however, such a mistake can cause you to catch your whole ski, with the pressure of the snow making such a recovery difficult if not impossible. As a result, you often end up taking an unexpected bath. But don't let that scare you away.

First, in order to properly ski powder, you must realize that it is much easier to turn your skis when you have gathered a bit of speed and momentum. In a way, powder skiing is quite similar to water skiing, since the faster you go (within the bounds of good sense, of course), the better your skis will plane and the easier they will turn. In fact, when you are going at a good clip in powder snow (assuming you have the right body position and technique), your skis seem to turn almost without effort. A second difference in skiing powder is that you must learn to keep your weight distributed evenly on both feet—as opposed to turning on harder snow, where you should tend to carry more weight on the lower or outside ski. Another good rule to keep in mind while skiing powder, particularly in areas where there may be hidden obstacles beneath the snow, is to keep your weight farther back on your skis than normal (more on your heels), so that your ski tips can plane above the snow. Rather than a conscious leaning back, I would think of it more as an avoidance of leaning forward, particularly by bending at the waist—a posture that will give you nothing but trouble and will increase the likelihood of burying your ski tips in the snow— with the often pleasant reward of an unexpected but inevitable somersault! You should also be aware that it is much easier to turn your skis in powder when you employ more than normal up-and-down motion (up-unweighting) with your body. This, of course, is due to the fact that the platform from which you unweight is much softer than hard snow, making subtle unweighting more difficult, if not impossible. Remember that this unweighting is brought about primarily by a flexing of the knees, not the waist, and not by a bobbing up, down, and every which way with the upper body, as is unfortunately the case with far too many of us.

The poles play a particularly important part in this unweighting, and that is why you see an exaggerated amount of arm movement on the part of powder skiers. It is also particularly important when skiing in powder that you carefully observe our previous advice regarding the importance of keeping your arms (and hence your upper body) forward and pointed down the fall line, especially during a series of turns. The reason why this is particularly important in this situation is simple: Once you get into trouble in the powder—and you will if you let your arms get behind—it becomes much more difficult to correct your mistake, often making it only a matter of time before you catch an edge and leave the rest to chance.

People often ask me whether it is necessary for them to buy special deep-powder skis in order to become a good powder skier. Unless you are a hard-core powder skier—the type who lives in a place like Alta, Utah, and skis the powder nearly every day—my answer is no. Provided you have done your homework as far as technique is concerned, any recreational ski with a relatively soft flex should get you through with flying colors. For years we thought that an extra-long and supersoft ski was needed in powder snow, but we have recently found that this is simply not the case. In fact, I have discovered that for me the most delightful skis to use in the deep stuff are the new short or compact skis.

1

2

3

4

SKIING THE POWDER

Don't be afraid to ski fast when you are in the powder; you need that speed so that your skis will plane above rather than dive under the snow surface. In the photos above, I have ventured off the beaten path for some really deep powder, and as you can see, I have been quite successful. The powder in the sequence is relatively heavy and ranges between two and three feet in depth. In photo 1, I have just completed a sweeping right-hand turn into the woods and raised my left arm and compressed my knees for the more than average up-unweighting it will take to shift into position (photo 2) for the next turn to my left. Note in this sequence how I have kept my weight back (by bending my knees and dropping my seat, not by bending forward at the waist), and yet, through my forward arm position, have managed to keep my upper body facing more or less down the fall line and prepared for what's to come. In photo 3 I am completing my left turn, at the same time dropping back on my skis to prepare myself to blast through a small drift (keeping my tips up in case that drift turns out to be a concealed obstacle), and simultaneously coming forward with my right pole to initiate the substantial unweighting I will need to commence my next turn under these more trying circumstances. In photo 4, you see me at the moment of impact with the drift. Although it is difficult to see from this photo, I have shifted my weight far back on my skis by bringing my knees nearly to my chest to allow my skis to plane over rather than dive into the drift (and whatever may lurk beneath). Again, note the forward position of my arms and how they keep me in a position from which I can maintain constant control over my skis.

SITUATION 2: ICE AND HARD-PACK

Although we all yearn for the pleasures of freshly fallen snow, we must face the reality that unless we are fortunate enough to be located in one of those places with a continuous supply of fresh snow, most of our skiing is done on hard, often icy slopes. To ski properly under these kinds of conditions requires extra attention to fitness, equipment, and technique. It is no accident that the areas with the "worst" snow conditions (for example, the eastern United States, where they refer to hard pack as "eastern powder") produce the most knowledgeable and technically competent skiers. It's simple: You just can't fake it on ice and hard-pack, where the even smallest of technical errors are magnified to the point that they become obvious to even the untrained eye.

The first requirement in skiing on hard snow, particularly on ice, is that the edges of the skis must not only be kept sharp, but also sharp in the proper way. To provide maximum holding power, the bottom of the steel edges must be filed so that they are perfectly flush with the plastic surface of the ski sole. If that edge should protrude downward from the sole at any point, or be marred by burrs, these inperfections will slow you down and make it extremely difficult to carve a proper turn. The most important thing to remember is that the bottom of the edge should be flush with the bottom of the ski and form a perfect right angle with the sides. If the edge is not flush with the bottom within a degree of two either way, your skis will not perform as they were designed to. In the case of ice, your edges should not only be square, they should also be razor sharp if they are to exert their maximum holding power. You may test for sharpness by drawing a thumb or fingernail across your edges at various points along their length. If they are sharp, the edge will shave off a thin white film from the nail. If they are not, it is time to go back to the workbench.

If your equipment is adequate and your basic technique is sound, it is relatively easy to ski precisely on hard snow. The key to skiing on hard snow is a subtle increase in the bite of your edges by angulating— pushing your knees forward and into the hill while allowing your body to lean away from the hill so that your shoulders become more or less

1   2   3

ICE AND HARD-PACK

Although it may not seem obvious from these photos, I am making a high-speed carved left-hand turn on a very hard, icy snow surface which, as you can see from the large jump in the background, had recently been the site for a pro race. In photo 1, I am driving through a fast but gradual right turn and am about to unweight for the next turn. Note the forward and ready body position, with my right hand driving through the turn to keep my body squared over my skis, and also note the forward position of my left arm in anticipation of the next turn. At this point I would estimate that at least 65 per cent of my weight is on my left or downhill (or outside) ski. If you look closely, you will see that my skis are under a considerable amount of torque, which has caused them to bend to the desired arc of my turn. In photo 2, the stored energy of my previously flexed skis and my pole plant have virtually rebounded me into a neutral and totally unweighted position, from which it will be easy to set up for the next turn. Note in this photograph how the forward driving of my left arm is bringing the entire left side of my body (shoulder, hip,

knee, and foot) forward and into the proper position for the next turn. I should point out that it is not necessary to become airborne between these turns, and that it was due to underestimating the rebound action of my skis that I got into that position in this instance. Ideally, you should unweight just enough to allow you to shift into position for the next turn. Anything beyond that is pure showmanship, which may get you points in a freestyle contest but will surely lose you time on a racecourse. In photo 3 I have "touched down" and have begun to angulate (press my knees) in the direction of the turn and drive forward with my hands, hips, and knees to complete the turn. In photo 4 I have completed the cycle, simultaneously driving through my left turn and setting up for the next right. Again, note the forward and ready position of my upper body, always squared over the skis; the driving forward of my hands; the critical forward position of my hips to keep my weight over my skis; the angulation and forward driving of my knees, and finally, the pressure on and resultant torquing and turning of my skis, particularly the outside or downhill of the two.

THE CLASSIC CARVED TURN (below)

Here the photographer has captured me driving through a sharp high-speed carved parallel turn in the near-perfect form I wish were the rule rather than the exception. Note the quiet upper body—perfectly squared to the skis; the forward position of the hands and hips, and the forward and inward pressing of the knees. Note also that my gaze is not focused on my ski tips or the ground in front of me, but rather far (two to three turns) ahead, gathering the information I need to plan my route down the mountain and respond appropriately when I reach that point. Finally, take note that my feet are not glued together for style, but spread well apart for the stability that is so vital to good skiing, particularly on a hard or icy surface.

parallel to the slope. It is also of vital importance to keep your weight forward and over your skis throughout each turn. Generally speaking, your skis should be kept apart and weighted more or less equally, your weight pressing down over the whole of each foot, not just the toe or heel, thus allowing you to utilize the full length of each edge to bite the ice. Also, when skiing ice, you must carefully avoid applying too much turning power (counterrotation), or your skis will skid out of the intended track. Moreover, very little unweighting is necessary to initiate a turn on the ice or hard-pack. Once the turn has been started, you must rely on a subtle forward pressure by the knees and hips and the built-in turning action of the skis to complete the turn. To do this, you must keep the skis in the proper position throughout the turn, and keep the body positioned so that a maximum amount of torque can be applied to them so that they may perform that built-in function. The key: The hands and hips must stay forward, and the knees must drive forward and to the inside throughout the turn. Among other things, this helps concentrate most of your weight on the inside edges of the skis. If, under these circumstances, I find that my skis tend to slip out from under me, I press harder on my lower or outside ski, forcing its edge into the snow. If I still cannot hold and control my direction precisely, I know that I have to learn to live with their limitations and, if possible, reduce those limitations through an edge check and tune-up.

The two most common problems encountered in skiing ice and very hard snow are skidding and chattering. Skidding is usually the result of a combination of dull edges, insufficient angulation, and the weight not being properly positioned over the skis. Chattering—a rapid-fire succession of grabbing and releasing of the edges—can be caused by a number of things, but most often by an excessive leaning of the upper body into the turn, with the result that your weight is not kept over the skis throughout all phases of the turn.

For me, being able to properly ski on the hardest of ice is one of the greatest challenges of our sport. It is one of the greatest tests of technical proficiency and a frequently occurring situation that should be viewed not as an obstacle to avoid, but an opportunity to uncover technical flaws and improve overall skiing ability.

SITUATION 3: POOR VISIBILITY

In 1968, at Grenoble, I had to ski fast in the fog, but believe me, I don't make a habit of it. The conditions under which we ski, particularly in the high mountains, are quite changeable, and it is not uncommon for a skier to encounter two or more distinct and radically different climates in a single day or, in the case of the largest areas, on the same mountain at one time. Adverse weather conditions such as blizzard, rain, or fog obviously limit visibility, which in turn has a substantial limiting effect on your ability to take in the necessary input to ski properly. The basic rule for skiing in conditions of poor visibility is obvious, but not often observed: Don't outski your field of vision. Under such conditions, it is easy to lose all sense of direction, and even your sense of balance and movement. Let me tell you what happened to me. Several years ago I was visiting a ski area in New Zealand that I had never skied before, and although the mountain was enveloped in a dense fog, I felt it necessary to take a couple of runs to get a feel for the slope. Quite aware of the hidden dangers of skiing new terrain under conditions of poor visibility, I asked an instructor to point out a safe area to ski. He gestured to a practice area served by a T-bar and told me that I would be okay if I stayed reasonably close (within hearing distance) of the lift. I took my first run very slowly, staying within earshot of the lift. The fog was so dense that I could barely see beyond my ski tips. This, in combination with the water condensing on my goggles, made it virtually impossible to see where I was going. Although I was making turns, I had little feel for the snow under my feet. But for banging into an occasional irregularity in the terrain, I might as well have been skiing blindfolded on one of those revolving ski decks. Suddenly, as I drove forward to make a turn, I discovered no resistance. It felt almost as though I were falling through space—I was! This realization was slammed home when I crashed into the ground, coming out of both of my bindings and sinking waist-deep into very heavy, almost slushy powder snow, with the wind knocked out of me from impact. When I finally collected my breath, my equipment, and my senses, and dug myself out of my giant sitzmark, the fog had cleared enough to allow me to see that I had casually skied off a cliff, dropped more than thirty-five feet, and miraculously landed in a basin of snow that had accumulated between two very large and sharp rocks.

The best advice I can give when the conditions are this extreme is not to ski at all, but if you have to, make sure that you ski very carefully; that you have a thorough knowledge of the terrain on which you will be skiing (through actual experience—not a word of mouth); and that you are at all times well aware of your exact location. A good idea in such circumstances is to ski with a friend, both of you wearing bright dayglow orange anoraks, so that you will be visible to each other, the other skiers you may encounter and, if necessary, the rescue party. Another good bit of advice—one I did not follow when I took my unexpected *Galendaesprung*—is to stay close (but not too close) to a lift or something that you can use as a reference point.

The same rules apply to blizzards and heavy rain. If you ever ski in a rainstorm, beware of lightning, a hazard which mountain climbers know well and against which they protect themselves by divesting themselves of any metalic equipment that could attract a lightning bolt. This, of course, becomes less of a problem where you are surrounded by many higher points such as trees and lift towers, which will serve as lightning rods.

While I am on this subject, I should say that it is not only important for you to acquaint yourself with the terrain of an area you will be skiing, but also that you attempt to ascertain whether there exist any unusual characteristics or dangers you should look out for, particularly if you plan to venture off the beaten path. A few years ago, while filming the television series known as *The Killy Style,* I had the thrill of skiing the steep and symmetrical cone of the Ngurahoe Volcano on New Zealand's North Island. Before skiing the mountain, I learned from the local rangers (it is in the heart of a national park) that even though the mountain, with its snowy mantle, may appear invitingly skiable at all times, it can only be skied with safety during a two-hour period each day. If you ski it too early in the morning, it is a giant block of ice, and one fall will send you on a frightening, bruising, and abrasive slide to the bottom and likely disaster in the jagged rocks that encircle its base. If you wait too long, the snow will have turned to slush which, in combination with the steepness of the slope, can make for tricky, dangerous conditions and a formidable avalanche hazard. One additional hour, or an intervening cloudbank, and it will revert to a giant icefall.

Situation 4: Slush, Mush, and Other Such Slop

Those of you who have experienced spring skiing know that it has both good and bad points. On one hand, you have the pleasure of warm, sunny days where you can ski in your T-shirt, relaxed and yet so charged by the atmosphere that you feel you can do nothing wrong. On the other hand (like the conditions that prevail on the Ngurahoe Volcano), you must face crusty ice and frozen tracks in the mornings, slush in the afternoons, and a relatively brief period in between, when the happy medium of hard base and soft surface prevails. Although the ice can be difficult, it is the soft, deteriorated snow that poses the most difficulty and danger to the unwary, since it is rather easy to bury your skis and/or limbs in the seemingly bottomless soft snow. When the snow gets so soft that your skis begin to sink in, and there is danger of burying a tip, it is a good idea to sit farther back on your skis than normally would be the case (similar to powder skiing, but with a bit more caution) in order to keep the tips from diving. It is also prudent to ski with a lighter touch; to minimize the forward driving of the knees and thereby limit your chances of going over forward. As the snow gets softer, you should try to keep your weight distributed more evenly over both skis. Furthermore, as in the case of powder skiing, a more aggressive up-and-down movement will be necessary to properly unweight the skis and free them for the next turn. If, as is often the case in late spring or summer glacier skiing, the surface gets so soft that your pole plants find no bottom, it is time to call it a day and proceed very carefully down, negotiating the mountain through a series of traverses linked by hop turns, or if that is impossible, kick turns.

1

2

3

WIDE-TRACK TRAVERSE

I have found the wide-track traverse to be invaluable in getting myself out of sticky situations. In the sequence above, I use this technique to get me unscathed through a formidable rut and bank of wet snow. In photo 1 I have sensed the inevitable confrontation and have begun to prepare for the coming jolt by sitting back slightly and spreading my feet and arms for extra stability. As I hit the rut (photo 2), I am sitting even farther back, to prevent my ski tips from being caught by the bank on the far side of the rut, and at the same time am using my legs as shock absorbers to cushion the impact as I crash over, not into, this tricky variation in the terrain (photo 3).

SITUATION 5: *Wind-blown Crust:* A POEM

When the cold winds blow
over fresh powder snow,
there develops a crust
that your limbs it can bust.

It is not very strong,
and can't hold you for long.
If you're not fully wary
with conditions so hairy,
your tips you will bury
with results very scary!

So take my advice,
treat the crust not as ice.
Keep your weight fairly back;
it will give you some slack;
Keep your skis in their track
and together your act.

Above all, don't avoid it,
take shortcuts, or paranoid it.
Just be wary, and behind,
keeping good ol' common sense in mind.

by Jean-Claude Killy and Mike Halstead
on an otherwise uneventful summer afternoon
in Val d'Isere.

SITUATION 6: HIGH-ALTITUDE SKIING

Like the ocean, the high mountains are beautiful, but you cannot be an expert on them in just a couple of days. *Respect* should be your watchword in the mountains; they are much larger and more dangerous than you can possibly imagine. One of the obvious differences between mountain and flatland skiing are the rigors imposed by the relatively low altitudes. For example, my hometown of Val d'Isere, which particularly serious problem in Europe because, even though the mountains of the Alps are very large, the skiing takes place at relatively low altitudes. For example, my hometown of Val d'Isere, which is one of the highest mountain villages in Europe, is at a lower altitude than western Nebraska. Altitude does, however, become a fairly significant factor in the North American Rocky Mountains, where much of the skiing is done between eight thousand and eleven thousand feet above sea level. This, of course, is felt most acutely by skiers from lower areas who visit the Rockies for their annual skiing vacation. Altitude sickness most commonly manifests itself through shortness of breath, headaches, occasional dizziness, and an overall lack of energy. In my opinion, the best way to cope with this problem is to take it easy —to do everything a little bit slower, until you get acclimated. For reasons that I have not been able to figure out, I have never had a problem with high altitudes—even in the rarefied air of the Andes, where I scored decisive victories in the 1965 Chilean championships and 1966 World championships for that very reason. If your altitude sickness should go beyond mild fatigue and to the point of illness, it obviously is in your best interest to go back down to the base lodge and relax. It is surprising how effective just a day or two of relaxed living in the high-altitude environment is in combating this problem. Unfortunately (or fortunately, depending on your vantage point), everyone cannot live in the mountains, and a certain degree of this adjustment must take place on every trip to high-altitude areas. I do feel, however, that if you are in reasonably good physical condition (especially as far as lung capacity and your cardiovascular system are concerned), you will find this adaptation rather painless, if noticeable at all.

Another hazard present in the rarefied atmosphere at high altitudes is the high potential for serious overexposure to the sun. The sun is considerably more powerful at high altitudes for two reasons: First, there is less atmosphere present to filter out the powerful ultraviolet rays, and second, the snow around you acts as a giant reflector, increasing the number and angle of rays that reach your skin. Moreover, it is quite easy to be deceived as to the amount of sun you are taking in, since in the chill of the high mountain air, you often will not notice the burning until it's too late. The sun is our friend, but if we do not respect him, he can soon turn into a formidable foe. He can melt the snow and start avalanches; he can burn your skin and blind you; he can give you sunstroke and intense migraine headaches that last as long as two or three days. I think that now is an appropriate time to again recommend to you the value of good sunglasses because, believe me, snow blindness is no picnic. At very high altitudes, I highly recommend the use of "glacier goggles," powerful sunglasses with leather blinders that provide protection on all sides of the eyes. It is now fairly well established that overexposure to the sun is not only painful, but also can cause skin cancer and irrevocable premature aging of the skin. People often kid me because I never really look like a skier since I never have that golden tan. Believe me, there is method to my madness. Obviously there are precautions that can be taken to guard against the more severe effects of high-altitude sun. I suggest using high-altitude cream, zinc oxide preparation on the nose and lips, and even a sun visor when you are in the high altitudes, particularly in the late spring and summer. You may look like a peasant during the day, but you will feel and look like a king in the evening. What good is that hard-earned tan anyway if it comes off on your washcloth the day after you return to the city?

Just as you might accept the idea of getting your hair wet if you want to swim, you must learn to live with the fact that skiing is, in part, a constant flirtation with the cold. It is for this reason that many people avoid the sport, and this is unfortunate since, as any veteran skier can tell you, the warmth generated by the athletic activity more than compensates for the absence of heat in the skiing environment. However, as is true with the other environmental factors of skiing, one must be aware of the potential dangers of the cold and act accordingly to avoid them. The most commonly felt adverse effect of cold weather, and the one that can cause permanent damage to the body tissues, is frostbite. Perhaps the most ominous aspect of this potential hazard lies in the fact that one can become seriously frostbitten without even knowing it. The telltale sign of frostbite is a white hardened area of the skin. The first places stricken are usually at the extremities of the limbs and the areas of the face where there is more exposure and less circulation, such as the ears and nose.

If it is quite cold—that is, below ten degrees Fahrenheit, or warmer, but with a high "wind-chill factor" (a combination of temperature, wind speed, and humidity), it is a good idea to ski with someone (or check with your various partners as you ride up the lift) so that they can spot frostbite in its early stages. If this is not possible, you can check yourself by feeling for numb or hard spots on the face, ears, etc. If you do become frostbitten, it is important that you should know how to take care of it. The important thing is that you get out of the cold *immediately* and take steps to *gradually* thaw the frostbitten area. Many have found that immersion of the affected area, first in cold water, then progressing to room temperature, is an adequate procedure to this end. *Never* apply hot water to a frostbitten area, since the rapid temperature change can cause unnecessary cell damage. If you are the victim of severe frostbite (if the skin turns dark or feeling does not return to the affected area), see a doctor immediately.

As long as we are discussing the potentially hazardous aspects of the skiing environment, let's pause and pay our respects to that grandfather of skiing dangers, the avalanche. Avalanches most often occur when there has been a heavy buildup of snow on steeper slopes. The chance of an avalanche occurring is particularly acute when the sun has had an opportunity to work on this accumulated snow, making the surface snow heavier than that beneath. In many cases, the snow clings so tenuously to the mountain that a mere noise can be enough to trigger a major slide. There are several common-sense rules that apply to avalanches, the most obvious of which is that you should never ski in areas where there is a posted avalanche danger. The second bit of advice is that you should be wary of the conditions conducive to avalanches, even when skiing in nonposted areas. Fortunately, most ski resorts located in avalanche-prone areas have a competent ski patrol, highly trained in avalanche prevention, control, and rescue. If, in the mountains, you are shaken out of bed by an early-morning explosion, don't panic—it's the ski patrol blasting and/or shooting down potential avalanches.

Even though your chances of getting caught in an avalanche are quite slim, you should nevertheless be able to spot potential avalanche danger and know how to react in the event that one occurs. Some general rules:

- Never ski directly above anyone when there is potential avalanche danger.
- When skiing a steep, powder-covered slope where there exists a possibility of avalanche, it is a wise idea to ski with a friend, and one at a time, so if one person gets in trouble, the other will not be buried as well and will be free to go for help.
- It is a good policy to keep your ski pole straps undone when skiing in an avalanche area. For the same reason, I prefer ski brakes to safety straps in these situations.
- Don't make loud noises in avalanche-sensitive areas.

What if you do get caught in an avalanche? There is really no set response; you must use your best judgment based on the circumstances. Since avalanches can travel with amazing speed, it is foolhardy to try to outrun one. Probably the best policy is to unhook your ski pole straps and attempt to traverse out of the path of the avalanche. If it looks inevitable that you will be buried, reach down and unhook your skis and safety straps. Under certain circumstances, especially in lighter snow, it is possible to virtually swim your way out of the avalanche— or at least keep your head from being buried. If you feel yourself going under, double up and try to form an air pocket between your head, arms, legs, and chest. If you are buried, don't panic; you will only waste precious oxygen. If there is enough light to see, but you are not sure in which direction you should start digging, perform a gravity test by making a small snowball and seeing which way it drops. If it is not light enough for this test, let your spittle or urine show you which way to go.

If you are an *aficionado* of skiing out of bounds in avalanche-prone areas, there are now electronic homing devices available that will help others locate you if you are lost or buried. Another trick that has been employed from time to time by veteran deep-powder skiers is to trail a rope behind them, sometimes connected to a heavy-duty helium-filled balloon. Again, never ski out of bounds alone and without notifying the patrol, rangers, or other responsible parties of your planned itinerary.

Chapter Nine

SITUATIONS OF TERRAIN

While the previous chapter dealt with situations created largely by variations in climatic conditions, this chapter will address itself to variations in the terrain itself, variations created by nature and man alike that help provide the challenge and excitement that are skiing. In this chapter, we talk about situations that are frequently encountered at most ski areas and also special situations that can be sought out for variety and/or solitude. The purpose of this chapter is to make you aware of these varied situations and to show you the adjustments I make in my basic technique in order to turn them from obstacles to vehicles for further skiing enjoyment.

SITUATION 7: SKIING THE STEEP

Many skiers, even some very proficient ones, miss out on some of the very best skiing because they are intimidated or frightened away by the steep sections of some of the very best runs. Although it is certainly harder work to master a steep *piste* than it is to cruise on the flats, it is a feat that is not all that difficult from a technical standpoint, and with the proper approach, the steepest of mountains can be handled adequately—even by beginning skiers. Over the past few years, a breed of skiers has developed who have sought to prove that virtually anything can be accomplished on skis. These people choose to test themselves on some of the steepest slopes of the Alps, and more recently, even Mount Everest. One moment of poor judgment, bad timing, or physical weakness in these precipitous places could mean the end of a skier's life. Ob-

When the going gets tough, *don't panic*—even a novice can safely descend the steepest of slopes by maintaining a cool head and proper utilization of three basic moves: traversing, sideslipping, and the kick turn.

viously, not everyone wants to risk breaking his or her neck to prove that the world's steepest slopes can be conquered. Sometimes it seems enough just to be able to get down the steeper sections of those trails and slopes marked "expert" or "most difficult" by the ski areas. The way to proceed, therefore, is to practice on progressively steeper slopes, developing a few special skills for the steep and building your confidence as you go.

The primary difference between skiing a steep and a flat slope is that on the former, you must train yourself to ski more slowly, fully completing each turn and linking those turns with traverses to check your speed and keep it at a reasonably safe pace considering the circumstances. The first thing you should remember if you should ever "bite off a little more than you can chew" and find yourself cringing in terror, barely clinging to the side of a seemingly perpendicular precipice, is: *Do not panic!* Even if you are a novice, there are three basic maneuvers in your bag of tricks that, if properly utilized, will get you through the roughest of spots: traversing, sideslipping, and the kick turn.

Traversing

When traversing a very steep slope there are two main points that should be kept in mind. To begin with, your skis should be kept wide apart; first, because that position provides a wider and more stable base; and second, when it's very steep, you simply cannot risk getting the boots or skis entangled with each other just because you want to look good. I have also found it helpful to extend the arms sidewise from the body when skiing the steep (and other rough conditions). In effect you are using your arms as balancing aids similar to the pole used by a tight-rope artist. The second thing to remember is that you should keep your weight over your feet, with approximately two thirds of your weight on your lower ski. You don't want to chance having your skis slip out from under you because you are leaning into the hill or putting too much weight on your uphill ski. The risk, of course, is not in the fall itself, but in the fact that once down, you might quickly slide out of control, with consequences best left to the imagination.

THE TRAVERSE

The traverse is often a good way to get or stay out of trouble on the steep. Here I am using a traverse as part of my strategy of negotiating a very steep section of the mountain. Note how my knees are bent and angulated into the slope, with about two thirds of my weight on my downhill ski, enabling me to successfully resist gravity and maintain a firm grip on the mountain. Note also that my weight is over my skis, no leaning into the slope, and that my arms and feet are spread wide to provide more stability.

Changing Direction

While descending a steep slope, your speed will be directly proportionate to the angle of your traverse relative to the fall line. When you want to slow down or stop, merely increase the angle of your traverse away from the fall line. There are, of course, several ways to link your traverses: snowplow turns (very difficult on the steep), stem turns (also difficult), parallel turns, and kick turns. The choice will naturally depend on your level of competence and technical proficiency. If you are linking your traverses with parallel turns (and this should be the goal of every skier), there are two main things to remember: First, because of your slow speed, the amount of angulation you will need to hang onto the steep slope, and the angle of the slope itself, you will find that a great deal of up-unweighting will be necessary to enable you to swing the skis around and into position for the next turn. This unweighting is aided to a great degree by placing a considerable amount of weight on your inside or downhill pole and using that pole as a pivot point around which to make your turn. Obviously, if you are to remain under control, these turns should be of rather short radius—and completed. In many instances, you will find that you are swiveling, even jumping, your skis around rather than making clean, carved turns. Don't worry; the main goal is to get them out of the fall line and in the opposite direction as soon as possible, so that you do not get out of control. Although it is pretty much a matter of personal preference and style, many top skiers have found a double pole plant helpful in achieving the requisite amount of up-unweighting to initiate controlled parallel turns on the steep. If you do not have enough competence (or confidence) in your parallel turns to safety link your traverses on the steep, then you'd better play it safe and connect them with a series of stem or snowplow turns. If you are still nervous, then I recommend that old reliable: the kick turn.

Sideslipping

Another tool that can be invaluable in negotiating the steep, particularly in narrow passages where traversing and turning are difficult (if not impossible), is the controlled sideslip. When you find yourself on a steep slope, quivering in your boots, it should ease your mind to

THE KICK TURN

Although the kick turn is a basic maneuver that is taught during the first day of almost every ski school, it has subtleties that come into play if you want to execute it on a steep grade. On the flat, either foot (and ski) can be kicked around first. However, when doing a kick turn on a steep side hill, only the lower ski can be safely kicked first. As the lower ski is kicked around, you are in a most precarious position. If your upper ski slips forward, backward, or sideways, you could take an awkward, leg-tangling tumble. To guard against this, take the following precautions:

- Stand across the slope (perpendicular to the fall line) so that the skis will not move forward or backward as you execute the maneuver. To insure this, stamp your upper ski firmly in place (photo 1). ·
- Place your ski poles behind you, planted in the snow.
- When you kick the lower ski around, be conscious of getting a firm support from your two poles, upper leg, and ski (photo 2).
- Once the lower ski has been kicked around into its new position, be very sure to place it directly across the slope (photo 3) so that it will not move when you shift your weight to it in the process of bringing the other ski around (photo 4). Do not move your ski poles until you have brought both skis around (photo 5).

It is a good idea to practice this little maneuver while you are on the flatter slopes so that you will have confidence and be able to pull it off successfully when the going gets tough.

remember that you don't have to go straight down, or across, or make turns: You can always sideslip or skid down. Because the full length of your edges can be used to break your descent, sideslipping allows you to go fast or slow, at your discretion. If you decrease the angle that the bottoms of your skis make with the slope, the edges will lose their grip and you will slide sideways. In order for this maneuver to be effective, it must be executed from the same basic body position I have described above in connection with the traverse—that is, you should remember to keep your weight over your skis and not leaning into the hill, where you could easily lose your footing.

So, my friends, when you find yourself in a seemingly impossible state of affairs, remember: Don't panic! Survey the situation, and plan your strategy. A relaxed and concentrated application of the wide-track traverse, the parallel, snowplow, stem, or kick turn, and the side-slip; or, as you will most likely find practical, a combination of all of the above, should keep your mind off the potential dangers and take you safely to the bottom of areas where even angels fear to tread.

SITUATION 8: SKIING THE BUMPS

Bumps, or moguls as they are called in skiing, are, of course, the mounds of snow that are formed when many skiers take the same paths down the mountain. There are two attitudes that you can take toward the bumps: You can regard them as a nuisance or as an opportunity. Since bumps are caused by skiers, and the number of skiers seems to be increasing every year, I would recommend that you opt for the latter point of view.

As you probably know, bump skiing has become very popular among the younger generation of skiers. This form of skiing has become so popular in recent years that it has been institutionalized to the extent that it is now one of three events constituting the exciting new sport of freestyle skiing. In the "good old days," bumps were rather benign creatures, large enough to allow safe passage through a series of linked parallel turns in the gullies that separated them. With the advent of short skis and a subsequent generation of hot-dog skiers with their wiggle-waggle technique, the bumps have become smaller and more

1   2   3

5   4

THE FIRST APPROACH: SOAKNG THEM UP

One way to deal with bumps, particularly the smaller ones, is to absorb them by using your body as a large shock absorber. When you ski into a bump, there is a tendency for it to slow down your skis and for your inertia to cause the upper part of your body to pitch forward. To compensate for this forward jerk, you should bend at the ankles, knees, and waist and lean back slightly just before impact (photo 1). When you hit the bump, your object should be to absorb it, primarily with the lower body, keeping the head and shoulders quiet, thus preserving your sense of balance and keeping your weight over the feet (photos 2–3). The French term for this way of swallowing the big bumps is *avalement* (pronounced "ah-val-mon"). Ski tall (photo 4), ski small (photo 5), and adapt to terrain: Extend in the troughs, compress on the bumps, and you will find that it is much easier to maintain control when the going gets hairy.

pronounced, making it all the more necessary for the average skier to understand the various techniques that may be employed to cope with them. Generally speaking, there are a number of basic approaches you can take with the bumps, all of which become part of your strategy while skiing through a field of moguls. In this situation we will examine them individually; in Situation 9, we will explore two basic strategies of how to deal with them in the aggregate.

The Second Approach: Avoiding Them

In some instances, a bump will be so abrupt (or located in such a manner) that you will want to avoid it altogether. This can be done in two ways: by skiing around it or by clearing it entirely through what we refer to as a prejump. The concept of skiing around a bump is self-explanatory; the prejump is not, and requires a bit of explanation. The prejump is just what it sounds like—jumping before the bump. The idea is to lift off into the air before you get to the bump, clear it, and land on its downslope, or on smoother ground beyond the bump. To initiate a prejump, you lower your body position then quickly and powerfully extend your legs. Once the skis leave the snow, you pull the knees up toward your chest, simultaneously dropping both hands to your sides so that while you are in the air they are midway between your knees and your skis—even lower in the more exaggerated jumps.

Another, easier way to initiate the prejump (if the terrain permits) is to use the upslope of one mogul as a miniature ski jump to launch you into the air so that you may clear one or more of the other bumps. While you are airborne, it is important that you remain relaxed and keep your weight forward and over your skis. Once the obstacle or bump has been cleared, lower your legs to prepare for the landing, and use them as shock absorbers to cushion the impact. After some practice at prejumping, you will gradually build up to where you can confidently and safely leap over the largest moguls, landing smoothly on the downside of others.

3 2

1

4

5

6

THE THIRD APPROACH: USING THEM TO TURN

Although the bumps may appear to make turning more difficult, they can, if used properly, be turned to your advantage and help you to execute graceful, almost effortless parallel turns. One such turn, shown in the above sequence, is that which I refer to as the "mogul christie." Here is how it is executed: I ski to the mogul (photo 1), and as my tips pass the crest (photo 2), I plant my pole near the top of the bump, comfortably off to the side and, at the brief instance that my skis are balanced on the crest of the mogul (photo 3)—when the tips and tails are actually off the snow—I drive forward with my inside arm, using the top of the mogul as a pivot point around which my skis swivel with ease, since the only part touching the snow is the small area under my feet. Note that as I hit the bump, I lowered my hips somewhat to allow me to absorb the shock and give me an extra bit of unweighting so that I could move my knees to the inside of the turn. Once the skis have turned (photo 4), I move my hips up and forward (photo 5) to keep my body weight over the skis on the downslope of the mogul and enable me to finish a carved turn (photo 6), controlling the radius thereof by the amount of edging and steering I do with my knees and feet. This turn is not only easy, but as you can see from photo 6, it is hair-raising as well!

1

2

3

4

5

THE AIRPLANE TURN

Another way to use the bumps to your advantage in turning is the "airplane" turn, so named because when you execute it properly, you feel as though you are actually banking or turning on air. In reality, an airplane turn is but a combination of a jump off a bump and an ordinary parallel turn. Obviously, you cannot carve a turn in thin air. You can, however, use your unweighted state as you fly through the air as an opportunity to shift into position for the next turn. In photo 1 I am traversing to the right and wish to make an airplane turn to the left. I then co-ordinate a left-handed pole plant with my take-off from the bump (photo 2) and, as I fly through the air (photo 3), I use my arms for balance and fight to bring them forward so that my weight will be more over my skis when I touch down. Co-ordinated with this maneuver is a shift of my knees to the left (photo 4) so that when my skis are fully weighted (photo 5) I will be in a slightly angulated position, with my weight moving back over my skis and on the left or inside edges. Believe it or not, this turn is relatively easy to execute, a good way to change direction, at the same time clearing the rough spots, and, best of all, it's fun.

THE OVERALL APPROACH: SKI LIKE A CAT

Our previous conversation on the virtues of wide-tracking—skiing not with the boots glued together, but at least six inches apart—is particularly relevant when skiing the bumps. If you try to ski in moguls with your feet glued together, I think you will find that not infrequently you will cross your tips with little time to recover. This is quite understandable, since in a mogul field it is easy for one ski to be deflected into the other by an irregularity in the terrain or for the skis to want to take separate paths since, in such conditions, you are crossing many different angles of terrain, not necessarily with both skis at the same time. This is also an appropriate time to put in a plug for the utility of independent leg action. To achieve this, it is helpful if you can visualize your legs as two independent shock absorbers that constantly soak up changes in the terrain and make minute adjustments to keep your skis on the ground and in the proper line. No matter how you drop a cat, it always seems to land on its feet, poised and ready for action. With a relaxed and proper body position, widetracking and independent leg action, you will be able to ski with fluid stability—like a cat!

Situation 9: Skiing the Headwall

Most ski areas, even the very smallest, have their famous run—the one that is so steep it can "barely hold snow" and on which the bumps are so big that the skiers "can get lost in them." These runs, such as Sun Valley's Exhibition, Vail's Prima, and The National at Stowe, are generally considered to provide a test that, in chauvinistic terms, "separates the men from the boys." In reality, if you refuse to be intimidated by these monsters, and approach them strategically, and turn by turn, you will soon find yourself at the bottom with far less difficulty than you had anticipated. If you have paid attention to everything I have said to this point, particularly the materials presented in Situations 7 and 8, you should be able to conquer the most formidable of headwalls.

There are two basic approaches to skiing the headwall, the choice being determined by your level of technical proficiency, your physical condition, and how courageous you feel on that particular day.

Easy Does It

For lack of a better label, I will refer to the first approach as the "easy does it" or, if you will permit me this bit of artistic license, the "Clark Kent" approach. This option consists of picking your way down through the moguls, in essence seeking out the path of least resistance through a series of wide traverses, connected by carved turns around the bumps, bump christies, and/or airplane turns when the time is right. The main points to remember here are that during the traverses (which will make up most of your run), you should remain in a relaxed, wide-tracking position, with your weight over your skis (not leaning into the hill), the uphill hand slightly forward, and the legs working (sometimes independently, sometimes as a unit) as shock-ab-

THE "EASY DOES IT" OR "CLARK KENT" APPROACH

This is, in essence, a series of wide-track traverses, linked by round, completed parallel turns. Tackling a headwall is like running a marathon: If you think about the whole, you are finished before you start; if you take it turn by turn, you will be at the bottom in no time.

sorbing devices to keep your upper body still as you cross the slope. As you make the connecting turns, you should remember to pull your knees to the inside of each new turn, driving your inside arm forward and down the hill as you round those turns so that it does not fall behind and pull you into an awkward leaning position from which it will be difficult to recover when you hit the next bump.

Attack!

The second approach is the "attack" strategy or (please forgive me for this one) the "Superman" method. This approach consists of a series of linked turns (some actually on the ground) pretty much down the fall line, but with enough completion so that the skier maintains some semblance of control. The freestylers have an expression for this type of skiing: "Going for it!" Strong thigh and stomach muscles and a considerable amount of intestinal fortitude are important prerequisites for this type of skiing. A cool head and sound technique help as well. Here it helps to set up a rhythm and keep your eyes trained far ahead, planning the route you will take around, through, and over the bumps. Skiing the fall line of a headwall will usually involve sneaking your way down through the gullies that separate the bumps, periodically lifting off and "getting some air," and making airplane turns to avoid obstacles and with the purpose of getting back into the groove. Aggressiveness, a flexible lower body with shock-absorbing independent leg action, and a forward-facing and quiet upper body are musts. If there's one place to ski like a cat, this is it. There are two fatal flaws you must avoid if you are to make it to the bottom without mishap: First, never let your hands (particularly the inside hand) get behind your upper body; this will twist you out of position and invite sure disaster. Second, most of the shock absorption should be done with the knees and ankles, not at the waist. Bending forward or collapsing at the waist puts an unnecessary strain on the back, will subject your shins to a brutal pounding against the front of your ski boots, and worst of all, will set you up for an unexpected front flip.

The only way you will ever master the headwall is through practice, first as Clark Kent and then as Superman; not through a quick wardrobe change in a telephone booth, but through a metamorphosis that will take place as you become more confident and adventuresome.

1

2

3

4

THE "ATTACK" OR "SUPERMAN" APPROACH

The main things to remember when "going for it": Use your legs (not your waist) as the shock absorbers; control your speed by completing your turns; and keep your hands forward throughout, or your skis will surely run away from you. Oh yes, it's not a great idea to ski this type of terrain with your tongue flapping in the breeze—one fall could leave you speechless!

SITUATION 10: TRANSITIONS

Transitions are changes in the pitch of the slope that particularly if you encounter them at higher speeds, require an adjustment in the placement of your weight over the skis.

From Steep to Flat

In my downhill-racing days, when I would often reach speeds of eighty miles per hour or more, I had to anticipate transitions if I wanted to stay in one piece. However, it is just as important for you or me when moving along at much slower speeds to look ahead and anticipate what's coming up. Many surprises await the unwary. One of the changes in terrain that caused me many problems, ready or not, was the transition from a steep slope to a flat. As your skis go through the change of terrain, it feels as though your body is being compressed and you are about to be pitched forward onto your face. Believe me, that's just what can happen unless you train yourself to handle such situations. In fact, as we were shooting the sequence for this situation and were about to take some photos of me properly absorbing such a transition, an enthusiastic young skier (who turned out to be the cook at a restaurant at which we ate the following evening) came barreling down the precise spot where we were to stage our shot, pressing forward to stay on top of his skis, with little regard or adjustment for the coming transition. The result was comical, but could have been tragic had his bindings not released. As he hit the flat, both ski tips stuck in the snow, and to his great embarrassment (and our amusement), both bindings released, freeing him to make a full-frontal sitzmark in the soft snow of the flat. Unfortunately, our photographer was laughing too hard to capture the action, since it would have made a perfect example of how *not* to approach this type of transition. Needless to say, our friend rejected our request for an instant replay.

When you are skiing from a steeper slope to a flatter one, you must anticipate the transition, or your momentum will flatten you out and pitch you on your face, just as it did to our unfortunate friend. You can counter these forward forces by leaning back just before you hit

1

2

3

TRANSITION: FROM STEEP TO FLAT

the transition (see photos 1–2 p. 167) and absorbing the forward and downward pressures by bending at your ankles, knees, and waist (see photo 3 p. 167). Compress downward, but don't collapse. A similar situation arises when you go from faster snow, such as hard-pack or ice, to slower snow, such as powder. Again, you must anticipate this change by sitting back just before you hit the slower surface. Also, if you have time, and the transition appears to be too abrupt for you to negotiate straight on, you can greatly reduce its angle and severity by turning beforehand and entering it at less than a ninety-degree angle.

From Flat to Steep

Obviously the converse will be true when you are skiing on a relatively flat slope and come to a steeper one: You must learn to anticipate the sudden acceleration you will experience.

You do this by leaning forward before you get into the steeper pitch (see photo 2) no later than the time that your feet reach the crest of the drop-off. As you hit the transition, press forward (see photo 3) (not bending too much at the waist), and, if you are cruising at a fast pace, simultaneously absorb the shock of the crest with an up motion of the knees. Once you pass the crest, you should press downward (see photo 4) to keep your skis on the snow and under control. It is critical to the success of this maneuver that your hands be kept far forward, or there is a good chance that you will sit too far back and your skis will accelerate out from under you. Again, if the transition appears to be too steep to be taken safely head on, then it is best to turn beforehand and take it at an angle. This will substantially reduce the angle of the drop and the amount of necessary adjustment. A similar situation arises when you go from slower snow to faster snow, such as from powder to hard-pack. Again, you must anticipate the acceleration of your skis by pressing forward just before you reach the faster snow. Once you have completed the transition onto the steeper or faster slope, you can resume your basic body position.

1

2

3

TRANSITION: FROM FLAT TO STEEP

4

Crossing a Road

A third transitional situation (which is really a combination of the two we have just discussed) is that which is presented when you must cross over a road or a cat track. The first thing you should do in such a situation is to check to make sure that no skiers will be in your path as you cross the road. If you are going rather fast, and want to cut down on the severity of the road, you do so by turning before you hit the road and crossing it at less than a ninety-degree angle. If you are going fairly slowly, the road will present two distinct transitions—one from steep to flat, and one from flat to steep—and you need only apply the procedures we discussed above.

If you hit the road at a higher speed, your adjustment should consist of sitting back and extending your legs (see photo 1) to counter the transition into the flat (see photo 2), then quickly prejumping the crest (see photo 3), pulling the knees to the chest and dropping the arms down and forward to help get your weight in the proper position for the steeper slope below (see photo 4).

TRANSITION: CROSSING A ROAD

SITUATION 11: SKIING THE CAT TRACK

Cat tracks, of course, are the roads that zigzag up the mountain, providing access to the top for trucks and other vehicles during the summer and snow cats during the winter. They also provide a gradual descent down the mountain for the less proficient skiers and even an occasional exhausted expert. The main thing you should remember while skiing the cat track (beyond keeping an eye open for snow cats) is that it is intended in part as a safe means for skiers to reach the bottom and by no means (particularly when they are crowded) a place for fast skiing or horseplay. If you feel it necessary to stop, don't stop on the track itself unless you have no other option. Often you can stop by traversing onto the slope that continues up the mountain from the track. Think of the cat track as a highway for skiers. If you feel that you have to turn or stop to control your speed, make your intention known to the skiers behind you. A good rule is to keep to the right, letting the faster skiers pass on your left. This is a two-edged sword. If you are about to overtake another skier, announce something like "on your left," and do so with enough warning so that the other skier can react. If you do this too late, you might scare the other skier, causing him to turn the wrong way and create obvious problems for the two of you and everyone around you. Another important point to keep in mind is that cat tracks often intersect with busy trails and slopes on their route down the mountain, and it is a good idea when reaching such an intersection to slow down (not with a sudden turn, but with a snow plow) and take a glance up the trail to make sure you will not cut in front of an oncoming skier who, as we know, has the right-of-way in this instance.

1   2

It is always a good idea to check your speed and look for oncoming skiers when entering a larger trail on the cat track (photo 1). Also, cat tracks are most safely negotiated (for you as well as others) through straight running (photo 2), not slalom or downhill racing.

5   4

SITUATION 12: SKIING THE NOT-SO-RAGGED EDGE

Although I have delighted in the growth of our favorite sport over the past few years, this sudden popularity hasn't come without its problems. One of the most discouraging aspects of modern skiing, one that is felt most acutely by veteran skiers, and one that affects most of those who by necessity must ski on weekends or during holiday periods, is the tremendous increase in the number of skiers on the hill. Overcrowding, of course, carries with it two inherent sets of problems: problems caused by too many people trying to do the same thing in the same place at the same time, and problems related to the effect that too many skiers can have on the slope itself.

There is, however, one salvation. Skiers, like most people, tend to follow the herd, congregating on certain favored runs and taking the same route, usually down the center. One fairly obvious but seldom-utilized way of avoiding the traffic jam and ravaged slopes is to ski along the edges of crowded slopes. In fact, you will be positively amazed to find how smooth the going is along the borders of even the

3

2

1

SKIING THE SIDES

In photo 1, I am completing a left turn against the bank of snow that has accumulated at the edge of the trail, and am about to plant my right pole in anticipation of a right turn against a mogul. Note the forward position of my arms: the left hand driving forward, keeping my body in position to complete my left-hand turn, my right hand forward for the pole plant that will initiate the up-unweighting that I will need to shift into

position for the coming right-hand turn. The snow flying from my skis illustrates two points: There is good snow left at the side of the trail, and I am driving forward hard (with my ankles, knees, and hips rather than at the waist) to complete my turn and thereby control my speed. In photo 4, I have completed my pole plant and am driving forward (keeping my arms forward) into a left-hand turn against the bank. Building up too much speed (photo 5), I drive forward with extra force, making a more complete turn to the center (not the edge) of the slope to check my speed.

most congested of trails. My basic strategy when skiing a trail's edge is to make a series of linked, carved turns, using the sides of the larger moguls and the bank that invariably builds up at the extreme edge of the trail as platforms on which to make my turns. One of the inherent dangers in skiing the edge (and the explanation of why the edges are smoother than the middle) is the possibility of the skier losing control and skiing into the woods. The risk can be minimized if you observe the following:

- Never ski out of control, particularly in situations where you do not have enough time to react.
- Start your turns early so that as you are approaching the woods, you will have begun the process of initiating your turn back onto the trail.
- Do not ski too close to the edge, since there may be dangerous obstacles hidden beneath the unpacked border snow.

SITUATIONS OF TERRAIN   175

SITUATION 13: SKIING THE GLADES

How many times have you arrived at a ski area only to discover that you had "just missed" some of the best powder skiing of the season? Even more frustrating are those times when long Friday-night drives to the area, a malfunctioning alarm clock, a fun but taxing evening of *après*-ski activities, or a last-minute adjustment to your equipment keep you off the slopes during that crucial first hour of a fresh snowfall. The way I cope with this problem is simply to get off the beaten path. My first strategy is to ski the sides of my favorite runs and, if someone has beaten me there, to seek the less popular runs. When it appears that the whole mountain has been well traveled, it is the time for a new and exciting adventure: skiing the glades.

By "glades" I mean those areas where the forests have been cleared to the extent that there is enough space between the trees to accommodate skiers. Since these areas are seldom skied and their trees provide shade that preserves the lighter snow, they can provide some extraordinary powder skiing—days, even weeks after a snowfall, when soft snow is just a memory on other parts of the mountain. The glades provide further adventure in that they present somewhat of an obstacle course—a natural slalom, if you will. With the pleasures of skiing the glades come the responsibilities, and I would recommend that you keep the following in mind:

- Be alert and keep your eyes trained well in front of you to spot potentially dangerous obstacles such as stumps, rocks, or fallen trees.
- Never ski into blind areas.
- Never ski out of bounds—that is, beyond the posted areas—without first checking with the area ski patrol.
- Make round, completed turns around the trees, and ski under control so that you will be able to convert those round turns into a stop at a moment's notice.
- Do not ski too close to the base of the trees. The trunk or foliage of the tree absorbs heat from the sun and in many cases may camouflage an indentation surrounding the tree, which can catch your ski and pull you into it.
- Whenever you ski the glades, ski with a friend. You will never know when you may need help.

1

2

3

SKIING THE GLADES

In these photographs I have decided to ski off the beaten track and into the glades in search of fresh snow and new adventure. Note how my weight is slightly back of center to facilitate the planing of my ski tips in the softer, relatively bottomless powder snow. In photo 1, I am in the process of completing my turn around (and a safe distance from) a large evergreen. Note that I have kept my inside (left) hand forward throughout the turn and that I have my right hand forward so it will be ready to initiate my next right-hand turn, my upper body facing downhill in anticipation of my next turn. In photo 2 I have compressed my body and readied my right hand for the pole plant that, along with the uncoiling of my body, will give me the necessary unweighting to shift into position for the next turn. In photo 3 I am totally unweighted and about to move forward into my next turn. Note that although my weight is back and my skis are jetting forward, my forward arm position has kept me over my skis, balanced and under control.

SITUATION 14: SKIING THE GULLY

As you can see from this photograph, there are two ways to ski a gully: down the center or banking off the sides. I have found that I enjoy the latter for several reasons. First, people have a tendency to crowd the bottom of a gully and ski back and forth, creating a washboard surface, which can be a most unpleasant experience for a faster skier. By skiing the sides of the gully, you can avoid the crowds and the rough surface in between. One exciting aspect of gully skiing is that you can ski fast down one side and up the other, utilizing the up slope to control your momentum. Another is the additional thrill of banking, of using centrifugal force to allow you to bank your turns much as a race car rounds a curve on an oval racetrack. There are several things to keep in mind while skiing the gully: First, keep a lookout for other skiers—not only those skiing down the center, but also those who may be skiing the sides. The same gravitational forces that make gully skiing unique and exhilarating also have a tendency to pull skiers to the center, and it is conceivable for two skiers banking off opposite sides of the gully to meet head-on unless they are aware of one another and adjust their trajectories accordingly. Speeds, angles, distances, and an ever-changing fall line can be deceptive in gully skiing, and the pleasures of fast-banking turns bring the added responsibility of being alert and skiing under control. If you are skiing fast in the gully and suddenly lose it, the best way to regain control is simply to initiate a turn up one of the gully walls and hold it until you come to a stop.

For me, the most pleasurable strategy for skiing the gully is through a series of angled traverses across the gully floor linked by banking long-radius turns against the gully walls. If you carry the proper speed and maintain the proper body position (relaxed and squared over your skis), you will find that the walls of the gully will virtually make your turn for you. All you need do is ride a relatively flat ski and lean into the center of your turn, the amount of lean being determined by your speed and the angle of your turn and that of the gully wall. Too much banking will cause your edges to slip or chatter; insufficient banking could result in catching an outside edge.

1

2

SKIING THE GULLY

In photo 1 I am banking off the wall of the gully and completing a turn that will shoot me into a traverse across the gully floor. In photo 2 I have nearly completed my turn and am entering into the traverse. Note that I have kept my hands (particularly my inside or left hand) forward throughout the turn. In photo 3 I have completed a relaxed and upright traverse across the gully floor. As I begin to climb the slope of the opposite wall, I bring my right hand forward for the pole plant that will serve as the pivot point for a right-banking turn against the opposite wall. In photo 4, I plant my right pole and shift into my right-hand turn. Note here that I am slightly back on my skis and not leaning forward—a move that could prove disastrous when your momentum and centrifugal force begin to push you against the gully wall. In photo 5, I am in the middle of my turn, body relaxed with minimal flexing, my right hand coming forward through the turn. In photo 6, I drive through the turn with my hips, knees, and ankles, once again toward the gully floor.

4

5

6

Chapter Ten

NEW HORIZONS FOR
FUN AND IMPROVEMENT

If you have mastered everything we have discussed thus far, you are now an "expert" and are ready for just about anything. In these final pages I will touch upon some variations in the sport of skiing—some old and some new—that will add variety (and more fun) to your skiing experience, at the same time testing your ability and building skills that will have a positive spillover effect on all of your skiing activities. Once you become a proficient skier, a whole new world of challenges unfolds for you. We each push until we find our limits. Some, myself included, are not satisfied until they have probed the outer limits. Through my experiences on these fringes of our sport, I have come to appreciate the special considerations that go hand-in-hand with the adventure. Let us explore these so that if you too probe skiing's exciting outer limits, you will do so with enjoyment and safety and come back to tell us how it was.

SITUATION 15: ALPINE SKI RACING

It is widely thought that you have to be a superskier to race. Not true! Ski racing, if properly approached, can be as much fun for beginners as it is for experts. Witness the widespread popularity of standard racing—a series of fun races at localities across the land in which virtually any skier can race on a relatively easy course against the time of a local pro who has earned a handicap by skiing at the beginning of each year against the very best. Racing not only adds a fun new dimension to skiing, it also builds the essential skiing skills that are necessary for you to be able to handle all types of skiing situations. Racing teaches you to turn when you want to, not when it is convenient and, if you are to be successful, to make each turn an efficient, carved one. It is easy to gauge your progress—just look at your times. Moreover, racing, even at the most elementary level, is invaluable in developing the confidence and aggressive attitude that are so vital if you are to break through those real and imagined barriers and become a truly competent skier.

Some of you will say "No thanks, Jean-Claude, there is enough competition in this world. I ski to relax." Well, just let me say this: The competitive aspect of racing arises from your perception of the activity, not the activity itself, and if you consider the challenge to be against yourself rather than the other racers, you should find it more satisfying and compatible with even the most noncompetitive value system. In my opinion, racing is the quickest route to becoming an expert, and if you become better more quickly through racing, you will be that much closer to efficient, relaxed, and more pleasurable skiing.

Before getting into its technical aspects, let me say a couple of words about the various kinds of alpine ski racing. There are two basic types of skiing: alpine and nordic. While the two nordic events (cross-country and jumping) have their roots in the Scandinavian countries, the three alpine disciplines (slalom, giant slalom, and downhill) were first practiced in earnest in the high Alps of Europe.

Downhill

The downhill event began around the turn of the century—long before ski lifts were invented. It involved a contest in which several top skiers would start at the same time, each picking his route down the mountain, with the first one to reach the bottom the winner. This format grew increasingly dangerous as technique and equipment became more sophisticated, and it soon became necessary to time the racers individually, control their descent through strategic placement of poles (or gates), and devote an increasing amount of attention to course preparation. In 1936, at Garmisch-Partenkirchen, downhill, combined with slalom, became an Olympic event. Norwegian champion Birger Ruud was the victor in the first Olympic downhill event with a time of

4 minutes, 47.4 seconds. If you compare this with my 1 minute, 59.85 seconds at the 1968 Winter Games at Grenoble, it would appear that downhill has indeed come a long way. However, I think it is unfair (and a display of great naïveté) on the part of sportswriters to try to compare times from one course with another or even on the same course from year to year. Unlike rather standardized sporting events such as track and field and swimming, skiing conditions change frequently—even on the same course. For example, dangerous corners are eliminated, snow conditions are never the same, trees are cut out to make certain passages safer, and so on. I have mentioned these times only to point how much faster today's downhillers go. It is now not uncommon for a racer to be clocked at more than eighty miles per hour, and on several of the world's top courses, the average speed of the fastest finishers is in excess of sixty miles per hour.

Over the years, many competitors have been killed on downhill courses—not surprising when you realize how fast they go. The next time you drive your car at seventy miles per hour, try to imagine what it would be like on just two narrow skis—not on the highway, but rather on a steep, icy, bumpy course. Is it any wonder that downhillers must wear crash helmets and that downhill is considered to be the premier alpine event?

Slalom

The first slalom race took place in Switzerland in 1922 and consisted of single poles placed here and there on a slope to force the skiers to negotiate selected rough sections of terrain. This form of competition was championed principally by the British, notably Sir Arnold Lunn, the man who first drew up the rules and refined and promoted the event. A modern slalom course consists of fifty-five to sixty "gates," each consisting of two eight-to-ten-foot bamboo or plastic poles with either red or blue flags attached, set vertically in the snow thirteen feet apart. As is true with all of the alpine events, the slalom racer must make both of his feet and skis pass over the imaginary line between each pair of poles bearing flags of the same color. There are basically three types of gates: open, closed, and oblique. Open gates are set perpendicular to the fall line, closed gates parallel with the fall line, and oblique (or offset) gates positioned at any other angle to the fall line.

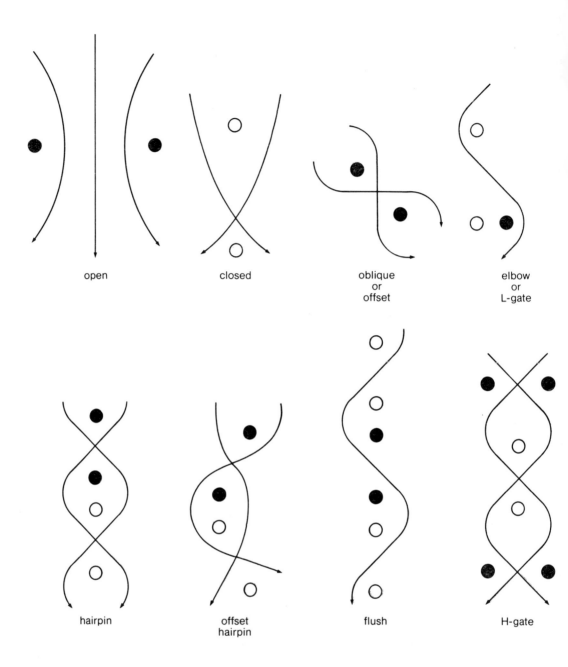

open   closed   oblique or offset   elbow or L-gate

hairpin   offset hairpin   flush   H-gate

Gates are arranged in various combinations, the most frequent being the hairpin, the offset hairpin, the elbow, the flush, and the H-gate. The diagrams above show how the poles for these various combinations would be set. The solid black dots indicate red flags; the open circles, blue flags. A world-class slalom event must be held on a fairly steep slope, with a vertical drop of at least 650 feet. Two courses are set, the racer gets one run on each course, and the winner is the person with the lowest combined time. Each course is usually negotiated by the top racers in close to one minute. A slalom racer's speed seldom exceeds thirty miles per hour. You can see why a slalom racer must be very agile, since he must make about one turn every second.

Giant Slalom

Giant slalom was a later edition to Olympic skiing competition. The first Olympic GS was held in 1952 at Oslo, Norway. Giant slalom courses are basically a compromise between the turny slalom and the high-speed downhill. A typical international class giant slalom will consist of roughly forty-five gates set on a mountain with a minimum vertical drop of 1,350 feet (as compared to 3,000 feet for the downhill and 650 feet for the slalom). It has often been said that of the three alpine events, the giant slalom is the best overall test of skiing ability, since it requires less of the acrobatics of slalom and the brute strength and courage of downhill, and places more of a premium on efficiently carved long-radius turns. It is on shorter (usually forty-five seconds or less) and relatively easy giant slalom courses that the various standard or "citizens" races are held.

Parallel Racing

For many, watching a slalom or giant slalom race is rather dull, since only one racer is on the course at any one time; and since the events are often won by mere hundredths of a second, it takes a very experienced eye to appreciate the subtle differences among the various competitors.

In recent years, parallel races have become very popular in these two events, especially among the pros. In these events, two competitors race each other, side by side through courses set as identically as possible. Both racers start at the same moment, and the first to finish his course is the winner of that particular heat. Then, to keep the competition fair, the racers swap courses and try again. The amount of time between each racer's finish is called the time differential. If racer A crosses the finish line 1.5 seconds before racer B on the first run, and racer B finishes 1.4 seconds ahead of racer A in the second run, racer A would be the victor by a combined time differential of .1 second.

Metal horse race-type starting mechanisms with simultaneously opening doors are utilized to insure that the racers leave the start at the same time. Often two or three large snow jumps are added to the course to make the action more exciting—and to provide space for sponsorship identification, of course! These dual races are customarily conducted along an elimination format similar to that used in tennis competitions. Believe me, dual racing is much more exciting to watch than the standard forms of alpine competition because you see who wins and *why*. It is very exciting to compete in as well, since you are always aware that the other racer is just ahead of you, or behind you, pressuring you to peak performance. This brings to mind a good point for you noncompetitive types: You should view your opponent not as an enemy, but as a friend, since by making things difficult for you, and you for him, you both get stronger and contribute to each other's progress in the process.

Although there is certainly not space in this book for us to present a definitive work on the subtleties of ski racing, we did feel that you might find the following tips helpful:

Setting the Course

When you set a course, the poles should be positioned in the snow so that everyone, from beginner to expert, can make it through successfully at his or her own pace. The course should be a series of smooth, linked turns. It should not be jerky or straight down the fall line. If you are the coursesetter, make sure that the poles are not too heavy, too brittle, or stuck too far into the snow. They should also be relatively smooth—with no protrusions that could pose obvious dangers to fast-moving skiers. Never set a course where it will interfere with others. It will do wonders for your peace of mind (and that of the ski area operator as well) if you get permission to set your course and conduct your race or practice sessions off to the side or on a run that is relatively secluded from recreational skiers. If that is not possible, the next best thing is to mark off the course with crisscrossed poles and/or a sign to warn approaching skiers. Once the course has been set, you should make sure that the snow surface is adequately prepared—that it has been firmly ski-packed and side-slipped, that it is clear of obstacles, and that the ruts are not allowed to get too deep. Obviously, common sense and courtesy dictate that you remove the poles from the slope and smooth out the ruts once you have finished. Never end a course without a proper runout, and if you set dual courses, make sure that both skiers finish in the same direction!

Some Helpful Hints

It is always a good idea to warm up well by taking at least a couple of runs before you ski the course. This also gives you a feel for the texture and speed of the snow on that given day. Before you run, study the course—not only the positions of the gates but the terrain as well. I guarantee that you will find racing much easier if you plan exactly where you are going and how you are going to do it. This planning must go on while you are racing down the course as well. It is the same kind of planning that goes on when a good skier skis for fun. I am referring to the importance of plotting your course, whether through a forest of slalom poles or a slope filled with moguls, by looking ahead, not where you are, but where you will soon be—in at least one turn, maybe even two. You must constantly look ahead for the exact spot to start your turn, the exact rut to avoid or make your skis follow so that your body will be able to react correctly once you get there. Otherwise, you will always be struggling to keep up with yourself.

Since the shortest distance between two points is a straight line, it follows that (at least on relatively smooth terrain) the fastest route down the race course is one that stays as close as possible to that straight line that connects the various gates from start to finish. One of my secrets for winning is that once on the course, I concentrate on getting my *skis* closer to the gates than anyone else. Once you know that you can cut your skis closer to the poles than the other competitors, you will have such confidence that you will be able to concentrate on other details such as getting a winning start and planning your finish-line strategy.

Of no less importance is the desirability of executing clean, efficiently carved turns rather than sliding the skis around the gates. The carved turns you will make on the racecourse are very similar to those you should be making in all hard-snow conditions. Remember to keep the arms forward and the hips and knees driving forward and into

You should try to get your feet closer to the gates than anyone . . . but not too close!

the turn. Remember, it is the knees, not the upper body, that should be moved in the direction of the turn. By leaning into the turn with your upper body, you will move your center of gravity away from the skis. This will contribute to unnecessary side-slipping and chattering, making it impossible for your feet to cut close to the gates, and keeping you from following the tightest and fastest line down the course. It is often with the knees that the best racers strike the gates when they are skiing a tight line, and it is for this reason that most of today's international-class racers protect themselves with knee pads. However, no one can escape the moderate degree of leaning into the turn that is necessary to offset the centrifugal force of the turn. To ski consistently close to the poles and yet not run them over, you must learn to duck around each gate by bringing your inside arm and shoulder forward on each turn. Don't jerk the shoulder forward, just lean it forward long enough to clear the pole and then resume your basic running position.

Another basic truth (from which you sometimes must deviate to accommodate unusual terrain) is that it is faster to anticipate—to turn before the gates—so that by the time you reach each gate, your skis are pointed toward the inside pole of the next gate down the course. By aiming straight at the poles and turning afterward, you will soon find yourself playing a game of "catch-up," which will haunt you all the way to the bottom of the course, where you will find yourself turning toward rather than scrambling for the finish.

In order to properly anticipate a gate, you must, at some point before your turn, get yourself above that imaginary straight line between it and the previous gate. One method is to follow a trajectory in which you aim slightly above each gate. The other is to aim directly at the inside pole of the gate and, at the last second, execute a step turn, a maneuver in which you step uphill with your uphill ski and, with a powerful plant of your downhill or inside pole, transfer your weight to that ski earlier than you would in a normal parallel turn. This can be accomplished through a very precise stepping up or by letting your uphill ski sneak uphill in response to increased angulation and forward pressure on the uphill edge. In either case, once the weight has been transferred to the uphill ski you must then roll the weight from that uphill edge to the downhill edge and drive forward into the turn. That is the hardest part of this maneuver, and you will have to practice hard and

1

2

3

4

SLALOM

In this series you see me charging through two gates of a tightly set single-pole slalom course. Note in photo 1 that although I have yet to pass the first of these gates, I have anticipated—completed my turn—prior to passing the gate and am heading directly toward a point just above the next gate. If you look closely, you will see that much of the torque of the turn is being stored in my heavily weighted outside (left) ski which, with the help of the next pole plant, will rebound and throw me into my totally unweighted position in photo 2. While I am still partially unweighted (photo 3), I will shift my knees into position for the next turn, most of which (again through anticipation) will be completed as I pass the gate. In photo 4 you see me frozen in near-perfect form, driving forward to complete my turn, and beginning to accelerate toward the next gate. Note the close proximity of my feet to the pole and how I have ducked my inside shoulder around the pole to allow this. Study this sequence carefully and take special note of the following: my basic body position (squared to the skis with my upper body quiet and facing downhill throughout the series); the placement of my weight (over my feet—not sitting back or pitched forward); the forward position of both arms throughout the series; the forward driving of the knees and hips; the direction of my gaze (not on the ground in front of me, but one or two gates ahead); and finally, my aggressive attitude.

long to perfect the skill. The remainder of the turn is accomplished like any other carved turn, and the skis are brought closer together to make it easy to get ready for perhaps another such step turn. Step turns (sometimes called "lateral projection") are most often utilized in giant slalom courses where you have more time to react between gates.

When racing, you should always remember that (at least in a traditional-type ski race) the clock is running from the time you open the mechanism in the starting gate to the time when your feet (or something large enough to trigger the photocell at the finish) pass over the finish line. I am convinced that many of my greatest international

THE STEP TURN

The step turn (or lateral projection) will allow you to follow the straightest (and fastest) line between two gates and, at the last second, step up and initiate your turn in anticipation of the next gate from the location you would have been in had you skied a higher (and slower) line. It is also a good trick to use in the event that you must quickly change your line—to avoid rough terrain or to get back into position after skidding low (or

wide) in a turn. In the sequence above, you see me using this maneuver to maintain the proper line in a tight section of a slalom course and yet maintain the forward speed that would surely have been lost had I tried to follow the same route by turning extra hard around the previous gate. Again, note the angulation, the aggressiveness, and the forward position of the arms, hips, and knees in these photos.

victories were won not because I was a faster skier on the course, but because I recognized the importance of a quick start and a fast finish.

The point to remember in a start is that you should try to get as much of your body moving down the hill as possible before your feet trip the starting mechanism. Second, you should scratch and scramble for that first gate. This will bring you to full speed as soon as possible and will set a tempo for your whole run. As you round the last gate and are heading toward the finish, remember that the race is not over until you have crossed the line. Tuck, skate, push with your poles—in short, do anything that will help you break that beam as soon as is humanly possible.

SITUATION 16: FREESTYLE SKIING

History

A child of the seventies with roots in the sixties, freestyle is, due to its spectacular nature, a popular crowd-pleaser and the fastest-growing form of alpine skiing competition today. Freestyle is something you do not have to study for years to be good at, but as with most exciting things, it can be dangerous unless approached with the proper attitude.

As far as I can determine, my friend Stein Eriksen got the whole thing started when he awed the skiing world in the early 1960s with his graceful front somersault. This Eriksen novelty soon evolved into a discipline known as trick or exhibition skiing, which became part of the skier's consciousness as the result of the efforts of maestros such as Art Furer, Herman Goellner, Tom LeRoy, Corky Fowler, and the irrepressible Rudi Wyrsch.

The next stage in the freestyle evolution can best be described as the free-spirit "hot-dog" phase in which ski bums, ex-racers, and local hot-shots would gather on the meanest, bumpiest run on the mountain and let it all hang out, rating each other subjectively, according to the relative level of excitement and overall hairiness of their runs. It was not long before promoters and other commercial interests saw the advertising and promotional values inherent in this new sport and forged it into the freestyle of today, a more objectively judged competition, consisting of three disciplines: moguls (or bumps—similar to the old hot-dog competitions), aerial acrobatics, and ballet. Each year, free-style has spawned new ski stars, many of whom come from diverse backgrounds not necessarily related to competitive skiing, such as figure skating, diving, and gymnastics. Let's take a closer look at the three freestyle disciplines.

Aerials

Without a doubt, the most exciting and dangerous freestyle discipline is the aerial acrobatic event. It takes time and painstaking effort for even the best athlete to build up to the point where he or she can safely execute the twists, flips, and other aerial maneuvers that make the sport so exciting to behold. In fact, even the top freestyle competitors work up to these complex aerial maneuvers gradually, first on trampolines with spotters and safety harnesses, and then on plastic-covered ramps pitching them into, yes, lakes before trying the real thing. Once they are ready to try their maneuvers on snow, they construct jumps according to very rigid specifications that will launch them in the proper trajectory, taking care to select a steep and soft landing area, since the incline will soften their impact on touchdown. With a flat landing, you might as well put on your gear and jump out of an upper window of a high-rise office building.

Bumps

The mogul event is one that you can practice by yourself on a mogul-studded hill—provided, of course, that you do not ski out of control and become a hazard to other skiers. When training in the bumps, make sure that the snow is not too soft, creating the likelihood of digging a ski tip. This type of skiing requires the longest warmup of any, since you must be very limber to absorb the shocks of the moguls at high speed. If you choose to "go for it" in an all-out run, then pick an empty slope or a special area, just as you would for racing practice. Also, the need for safety straps or ski brakes is extra urgent in this type of skiing, since the unpredictability of shock can often result in a lost ski; and since this event is usually practiced on a steeper slope, this makes for high-velocity runaway skis, which pose an obvious hazard to your fellow skiers.

Ballet

Although the ballet event is the slowest and most graceful of the three free-style disciplines, it poses a substantial threat of injury unless you are physically prepared and using the proper equipment, adjusted in accordance with the circumstances. Again, a good warmup with a lot of stretching is needed. As you might imagine, maneuvers with names like "outrigger," "helicopter," and yes, folks, "The Wong-banger," exert unusual torque on your limbs and torso. For obvious reasons, ballet skiing should be practiced on a smooth and gentle slope, and if you do not have ballet skis, you should use short skis with the bindings loosely adjusted before you try these pretzel-like maneuvers.

SITUATION 17: CROSS-COUNTRY AND TOURING

Because it originated centuries ago in Scandinavia, cross-country skiing can hardly be considered a "new horizon," but that is exactly the case with the many who in the past couple of years have found it to be a delightful and healthful way to retreat from the hustle and bustle of city life. Cross-country skiing can be as relaxing or as strenuous as you want to make it. Since you must rely on your own muscle-power to get along, your gear must be very light. The task of climbing uphill is made easy by special waxes that, when properly applied, allow the skis to glide forward effortlessly, at the same time preventing them from slipping back. Although in my opinion cross-country skiing is not as thrilling as alpine skiing, the former does have its compensations. To begin with, you don't need to spend money on lift tickets, and you can buy all the equipment you will need for under a hundred dollars. The cost is low because cross-country equipment is relatively easy to manufacture. Although the plastics revolution is now hitting the cross-country industry full force, the skis have traditionally been made of laminated hardwoods such as birch and ash. Though they run longer than standard alpine skis, they are often less than two inches wide and without steel edges. Cross-country bindings and boots are lighter and less sophisticated as well. The sole task of the binding is to clamp the front of the boot to the ski, freeing the heel to lift unimpeded so that you can make long, graceful strides. Once you learn the technique of cross-country (kick and glide), you can zip over flat stretches of snow with relatively little effort at speeds up to and exceeding twenty miles per hour. Cross-country ski boots are usually made of leather and cut very low, almost like a track shoe. The boot is fastened to the bindings by holes in the sole near the toes, which accept pins that stick up from the bindings. The last remaining item of specialized equipment is, of course, the ski pole. These usually extend to the height of your shoulders and are often made of special lightweight bamboo or aluminum, with a simple cork grip and leather strap for the wrist and a steel point at the tip curved forward so that it will slip easily out of the snow as you go gliding past.

Aside from the economic benefits of cross-country skiing, there exist the pleasure that comes from the thrill of mobility, and the satisfaction and feeling of well-being that accompany relatively strenuous cardiovascular/muscular activity. Perhaps the greatest benefit, however, is the aesthetic appeal of getting away from it all and truly enjoying the peace and quiet of the backwoods. Two principal variations of cross-country skiing are presently enjoying an unprecedented level of popularity. The first of these is classic cross-country skiing, which involves traveling over a prepared course, such as is done in the Winter Olympics. A recently popular extension of cross-country skiing is what has come to be known as touring, a wintertime equivalent of hiking (or, on longer trips, backpacking), which involves striking out into the wilderness, often for more than one day at a time. In ski touring, you use the same equipment as in cross-country, with the exception that touring skis are slightly wider (but still much narrower than alpine skis), to provide a broader base and to prevent you from sinking deep into the soft, untracked snow.

There are several things you should keep in mind when embarking on a cross-country adventure, particularly one that will involve long distances and/or camping overnight. First, plan your trip and let others know where you are going and how long you plan to be gone. It is a good practice to stick close to marked trails if possible.

As far as equipment is concerned, it is of vital importance that you get the right pair of boots. There are few things more unpleasant than a blister on the tenth mile of a twenty-mile trip. Most boots will feel good for about an hour, but if you go for two hours or more, the slightest irritation can become catastrophic. It is a good idea to wear warm but absorbent and well-ventilated garments. Natural textiles and wool are the best; nylon and rubberized fabrics are the worst, since you will easily become overheated and perspire.

If you are planning a longer trip, spend a little extra time planning. Since traveling over the snow on skis, particularly at high altitudes, is a physically demanding activity, it is important to be able to replenish your body with water and salt. I prefer to bring high-energy foods along on these occasions such as chocolate, nuts, and dried fruit. Moreover, you should take extra pains to bring sufficient clothing for any conceivable type of weather. A first-aid kit and compass are also indispensable equipment on a serious tour. By all means, observe weather forecasts. You may decide that you do not want to take that long trek after all or, if you do, you will know what to bring to meet any contingencies.

Before you embark on a long-distance journey, you should work up to it through a training program or several shorter trial runs. Always remember when on a long hike that there is always a return trip —unless, of course, you are headed in a circle! If your circular path was not intentional, chances are that you are lost. If this should happen (and I hope that it doesn't), don't panic, and keep active, particularly if it's very cold. Death by freezing involves several stages of discomfort, the last of which is a feeling of drowsiness followed by ———. Believe it or not, snow can be a great insulator, and if you are trapped on a mountainside or any other area with much snow and no shelter, a snow cave lined with pine boughs, if available, could be your ticket to survival. Once you realize that you are lost, don't waste energy wandering in circles if it is dark or foggy. If it is clear, use landmarks to set a straight course for yourself. If you are in the mountains, the best direction to go is down. If there are more than two people in your party —and this is a very good idea when long trips are involved—you can do as the veteran climbers and explorers do: One person can stay behind to make sure that those in front of him are walking in a straight line. Without such navigational aids, it is likely that you will go in circles. Generally we have one leg that is either stronger or longer than the other, and without visual reference points, we have a tendency to wander in a circular path.

In short, be careful when you start into an adventure. Remember the changeable nature of the mountains and that for each step you take and each hour you spend going out, you will have to exert the same amount of time and energy to return. I hope that this parade of horribles will not discourage you from sampling the delights of cross-country skiing or ski touring. Forewarned is forearmed, and a knowledge of the dangers involved and how to cope with them will make these exhilarating activities safer and more enjoyable. And please don't get the wrong idea: I consider these forms of nordic skiing to be supplementary to and not alternatives or substitutes for alpine skiing. In fact, I have found that both types of skiing complement each other quite well. Cross-country skiing helps develop the balance and stamina so important to good alpine skiing, while alpine skiing helps develop the muscular strength and technical skills so valuable in the downhill portion of cross-country skiing.

SITUATION 18: SKIING THE GLACIERS

High-altitude skiing, particularly in the spring or summer, when much of the seasonal surface snow is melted away, often involves skiing on glaciers. Of the various situations available in skiing, glaciers are the areas that I fear and respect most. I have come to know glaciers reasonaby well over the years, since we ski on glaciers quite often in Europe, particularly in the latter parts of the season.

Since glacier skiing is really a combination of skiing and mountaineering, and since glaciers contain many pitfalls not present in ordinary skiing, I advise taking along an experienced guide. The one thing you can assume while skiing the glaciers is that it is unsafe to make assumptions. You should remember that a glacier is really a great river of ice, constantly moving and changing in response to gravity, and that each time you ski it, it can be like skiing on a completely different slope.

I once had an experience that taught me the foolishness of making assumptions while on the glacier. I was skiing with a group of friends on Mount Blanc, and we stopped to rest and to have some refreshments at one of the mountain huts that serve as refuge to the many climbers who scale that massive peak each year. With the assumption that the area immediately around the hut would be safe (why else would they have built it there?), I strolled about with my skis over my shoulder when suddenly my feet broke through the crust and I fell into a narrow crevasse. Fortunately, almost miraculously, the crevasse was narrow enough so that my skis caught on either side, leaving me hanging from them by one arm with my feet dangling in the air. To you that might seem like a comical scene from a W. C. Fields movie. For me it was a nightmare and very nearly my final act. In glacier skiing, crevasses, snow bridges, and cornices can all present traps for the unwary unless you treat them with awareness and respect.

SITUATION 19: HELICOPTER SKIING

What person who considers himself to be a serious skier hasn't dreamed of having the opportunity to ski miles upon miles of feathery light-powder snow without the aggravation of lift lines or competition from a number of other skiers? Today, thanks to the helicopter and a growing number of entrepreneurs offering back-country powder-skiing adventures, this utopian vision is becoming reality for an increasing number of skiers each year. In the late spring, when most of the ski areas become unskiable due to warm weather, a significant number of hard-core enthusiasts head for the high *pistes,* where the snow is still of a consistency similar to that found at lower altitudes during the coldest winter months. In North America, mountain ranges with names like Bugaboo, Caribou, and Monashee have become almost legendary for their ability to provide this ultimate skiing experience. Since helicopter skiing involves deep-powder skiing at high altitudes, often upon glaciers, the skier should be vigilant against the hazards we discussed in connection with those types of skiing. Furthermore, although it seems so obvious that it should not have to be written, special care should be exercised *at all times* around the helicopter itself. Not long ago, near Tignes, France, an experienced 'copter pilot, in a rush to find a secluded place to relieve himself, scurried forth (bending at the waist to avoid the large propeller on the top of the helicopter) and ran directly into the rear prop, with results best left to the imagination. If this can happen to an experienced alpine pilot, it could happen to you as well if you do not exercise requisite diligence.

SITUATION 20: HANG GLIDING

Although I may be getting a bit far afield, I do feel that before bidding you *adieu,* I should devote a few sentences to an exciting new activity that many young skiers are trying and in which an alarming number are dying.

Hang gliding—riding the winds strapped to a larger version of a child's kite—is one of the easiest sports to do and at the same time one of easiest in which to kill yourself. This sport is without a doubt one of the most dangerous activities on the face of the earth—so dangerous, in fact, that after trying it several times with great success and much enjoyment, I quit. The primary difference between this sport and others is that you are almost totally at the mercy of forces beyond your control. For example, you can be in perfect control of a kite and suddenly hit a downdraft and drop one hundred feet—not a very pleasant prospect if you are only seventy-five feet above the ground! In this sport you can *never* be an expert. Perhaps it is because I have lost more than one close friend to this sport that it seems for me to have an untenable rate of mortality. Those who are killed seem to fit into two groups: beginners without proper instruction and/or proper equipment, and "experts" who get bored with short flights and, like Icarus, go one step too far, with their ultimate high becoming their ultimate downer. If, after pondering this collection of morbid thoughts, you still must fly, please take some bits of advice from one who has taken some pretty exciting rides and come back to tell of them.

First, I can think of few activities where it is more important to spend those extra couple of dollars to get the best possible equipment. It is wise to buy your kite from a proven maker, obtaining your brand advice from an instructor rather than one of those many "experts" you find practicing the sport.

Second, take lessons, not from an "expert," but from a certified instructor in one of the many professional hang-gliding schools that are springing up in many areas. Please don't think that you are an expert after two or three flights. Even the best have had some very unpleasant surprises. You should appreciate that you are, in reality, the pilot of a very small aircraft, with little or no protection for your body, and recognize that a working knowledge of aerodynamics, thermodynamics, and other characteristics of our atmosphere is vital. I happen to be a licensed airplane pilot and still find these elements most unpredictable. In fact, most pilots with whom I have discussed this subject are outspoken opponents of hang gliding. I believe that it is only a matter of time, and a short amount of time at that, before hang gliders will be treated as pilots and required to undergo a rigorous training program before they are allowed to fly.

You should always, *always,* have a flight plan and check list before every flight. Each pole, screw, stitch, cable, fitting, and square inch of fabric should be checked—no, *scrutinized*—before each and every flight. Provided that you know what you are doing once you are in the air, the work you do before the flight is more important than the flight itself—the preflight work could spell the difference between a pleasant experience and a dangerous and perhaps violent and tragic one. Never be afraid to call off a flight if weather conditions change.

Mandatory gear should include strong boots if you are not taking off on skis; strong gloves, since a bad landing often involves using your hands as part of your landing gear; strong pants—perhaps leather, since your knees can also form part of the landing gear; and if you feel that you have something upstairs worth saving, an approved crash helmet.

Part of your planning should include selecting a safe landing area and a working knowledge of the local topography should your flight not go exactly as planned. At the very least, know the areas you must avoid such as high-tension wires, highways, and bodies of water. It is always wise to determine the local rules in the area you plan to fly. In Val d'Isere, for example, there are only two mountains from which you can legally fly, and limited areas in which a landing is permissible.

Also, never take off behind another flier, since there is turbulence in his wake, which can cause you severe problems. Believe me, I know —this happened to me when the air current of a fellow flier twisted me to one side just enough that my skis hit, but fortunately did not catch on, a Poma lift cable.

Although there are many more things I could say regarding this subject, I will close at this point, for I do not want you to take this short section to be a definitive set of instructions on hang gliding. If you must take up this sport, my best advice can be summed up in two words: Take lessons. If you already fly: Take care!